West Meets East

Stories of Americans in China

WILLIAM N. BROWN

West Meets East: Stories of Americans in China

Photos throughout the book are used courtesy of the individuals and families featured in the respective chapters where the photos appear.

Library of Congress Control Number: 2026902823

CPSIA Code: PRV0226A

ISBN-13: 979-8-89138-825-3

Printed in the United States

Many thanks to my friend, Professor Hu Min, founder of New Channel International Education Group, for suggesting I write this book, for his encouragement and guidance, and for overseeing its translation.

Contents

Preface

> "The one thing I know about China is I will never know China; it's too big, too old, too diverse. That's the joy of China, the certain knowledge that even if I dedicated my life to learning about China, I die mostly ignorant."
>
> —*Anthony Bourdain*[*]

Like many of the Americans in this book, I had zero interest in China as a youth—and once I visited, I found it hard to leave. My two-year stay in China has now extended into its thirty-fifth year and counting. But that's nothing compared to the Caldwells of Tennessee, whose family stayed in Fujian for four generations and whose descendants visit to this day.

John Godwin, an international educator who has taught in numerous countries over his fifty-year career, said China was the only country in which he did not feel culture shock. Even more, he said his school board at Xiamen International School was the best he'd ever worked with, even though he spoke no Chinese and most of them did not speak English. He's seen the world,

* "Anthony Bourdain Parts Unknown," Shanghai, CNN, September 28, 2014, transcripts.cnn.com

but only China has he called his "second home."

Americans' affinity for China is nothing new. For the past two centuries, the United States has, overall, had a better relationship with China than have most Western nations. Granted, our leaders have made many mistakes (what nations' leaders have not, whether through ignorance or pursuing vested interests?). But the US was the first Western nation to stop our opium trade; we helped halt the insidious coolie trade; we invested heavily to modernize Chinese medicine and education (including helping to establish Tsinghua University); we tried to stop Europe from partitioning China into colonies as it did in Africa; we spent billions (in today's money) to arm China against Japan; and American volunteers in the Flying Tigers sacrificed their lives fighting side by side with the Chinese against impossible odds. And President Franklin Delano Roosevelt—in spite of his ancestors building their wealth on China opium—opposed Western colonialism toward China, and hoped for China to not only survive but thrive as a world power and a force for peace.

China-US relations have certainly had their ups and downs, but one constant has been that when Chinese and Americans get to know each other on a person-to-person level, they often become friends because they realize that our similarities outweigh our cultural and political differences. As the Chinese saying goes, we are all *hé ér bùtóng*, "alike but different." Once we see how we are alike—our common ground, *hé*—we can better understand, accept, and even embrace our differences, *bùtóng*.

Sometimes, our people-to-people relationships exert even national influence. Nixon travelled to China, for example, after an American ping pong player in China boarded the wrong bus and befriended a Chinese ping pong player—hence the term "Ping-pong diplomacy."

In November 2023, President Xi Jinping underscored the value of people-to-people relationships when he met President Biden at the Asian-Pacific Economic Cooperation (APEC) forum in San Francisco. President Xi proposed a new vision of "jointly working to build the five pillars of China-US relations," namely, to "jointly develop a right perception, manage disagreements effectively, advance mutually beneficial cooperation, shoulder responsibilities as major countries, and promote people-to-people exchanges."* He also stressed that "the hope of the China-US relationship lies in the people, its foundation is in the two societies, its future depends on the youth, and its vitality comes from exchanges at subnational levels."†

President Xi's speech was warmly welcomed by those of us keen on friendlier China-US relations, including by my good friend, Professor Hu Min, the famous international education expert and chairman of New Channel International Education Group. Hu Min promptly suggested we publish a collection of stories showing friendships forged by Americans living in China. "Great minds think alike!" I said. For almost twenty years, I had been collecting stories of nineteenth- and twentieth-century Americans in China, even going so far as to track down and interview their descendants in the US. Thanks to Prof. Hu Min's

---

* "An Overview of the Meeting Between Chinese and US Presidents in Lima by Foreign Ministry Spokesperson," News, Ministry of Foreign Affairs The People's Republic of China, last modified November 17, 2024, https://www.fmprc.gov.cn/eng/xw/fyrbt/202411/t20241117_11527715.html#:~:text=During%20the%20meeting%20in%20San,five%20pillars%20of%20the%20mansion.

† "Xi Jinping Sends Message to the 'Shared Journey of Friendship' US Youth Exchange Delegation," The Ministry, Ministry of Foreign Affairs The People's Republic of China, last modified July 2, 2024, https://www.fmprc.gov.cn/eng/wjb/zzjg_663340/bmdyzs_664814/xwlb_664816/202407/t20240717_11455227.html.

encouragement and support, I hope these stories of Americans in China, including a few contemporary Americans, will help increase our confidence in future China-US relations.

By researching people like General "Vinegar Joe" Stilwell, or interviewing people like headmaster John Godwin, entrepreneur Rob Bailey, and two-time Emmy winner (and two-time Oscar nominee) Chris Bremble, I've learned that what wins Americans' hearts is not the place but the people.

Americans resonate with Chinese because, in spite of cultural or political differences, we are all dreamers. Americans have "The American Dream," coined by James Adams in his 1931 bestseller, *The Epic of America*, and Chinese have "The China Dream," a phrase that President Xi Jinping has popularized.* Although Americans and Chinese differ somewhat in how we pursue our dreams, the dreams are essentially the same: a better life for our family and descendants, security, and peace.

And Chinese and Americans have long had good reason to pursue their dreams together. On July 4, 1891, Shao Youlian (邵友濂), governor of Fujian and Taiwan, visited Xiamen and made a heartfelt toast to celebrate America's Independence Day. *The Chinese Recorder* reported his "remarkable speech, which shows his intelligence, and suggests some things worthy of consideration."

Governor Shao concluded his toast with:

> No matter what happens, it needs no prophetic gift to know that the twentieth century will see at the forefront of the nations of the world China in the East and America in the West. Well may we pray that, for the welfare of

* "Potential of the Chinese Dream," *China Daily*, March 3, 2014.

humanity, their purposes will be as peaceful and upright as today.*

Sadly, the twentieth century's so-called Great Powers were neither peaceful nor upright, and so far, the twenty-first century is not much better, but there is hope—and it lies in people like you and me.

A key strategy to easing conflict is to stop demonizing the enemy by personalizing them. For example, during my two years in the US Air Force in Taiwan from 1976–1978, I was quite willing to fight the "Red Peril" only a hundred miles across the Taiwan Strait. But my life took a turn when a Mainland propaganda balloon dropped dozens of leaflets literally right on my head. I could not read Chinese, and would not have believed it if I could, but I was shocked that the Mainland's farmers in the photos looked just like my close friends in the Taiwan countryside. Until that point, I had never considered people on China's mainland as people—as sons, brothers, husbands, fathers, grandfathers, friends.

I determined then that someday I'd visit China's Mainland to see the truth for myself.

Since moving to Xiamen with my wife and two small sons in 1988, I've travelled over 200,000 km around the country, from Xiamen on the coast to Inner Mongolia in the North and Tibet and Xinjiang in the West. I've witnessed firsthand amazing successes, and also some missteps. But this is not surprising, given the historically unprecedented scope and pace of changes. Yet in every case, China learned from its mistakes and pressed on. But for me, as with many of the people in this book, what touched my heart and head the most was the people I've met—beginning

* "China's Power," *Chinese Recorder*, Vol. 23, p. 18, January, 1892.

with the poor teachers who shared their food rations when they did not even have enough for themselves.

In the last chapter, I will very briefly share the one "American in China" story that I'm most familiar—my own.*I hope this book's stories of Americans in China will encourage you to visit for yourself because today, as in 1891, the two great powers are still China in the East and the US in the West, and we still have so much to gain if we work together—and the entire world has much to lose if we do not.

See you in China.

* I share my three-decade story in greater depth in my books, *Off the Wall: How We Fell for China* (Foreign Languages Press, 2018) and *Thirty Years in Xiamen University: China's Most International University* (Xiamen University Press, 2021).

CHAPTER ONE

Introduction

"Kuliang, Ah! Kuliang"

I was surprised when a group of Americans visiting Fuzhou's Kuliang Mountain in July 2023 received a welcome letter from Xi Jinping. Even though I had corresponded with some of them for fifteen years, it turned out that Xi Jinping had known them twice as long as I had.

Upon landing in Fuzhou, some of the Americans said in fluent Fuzhou dialect, "Home!" But Fujian was also home to Xi Jinping for over seventeen years, and he wrote in his welcome letter:

> I hope that you will continue to write the Kuliang story and carry forward the special bonds, so that the friendship between our two peoples can stay forever strong and robust like the thousand-year-old cedar trees of Kuliang.

I was not surprised that Xi Jinping was so familiar with Kuliang's rich history as an international community of both foreigners and Chinese. Xi has always studied the culture and history of the places he has served, and when he moved to Fujian in 1985, he researched its rich history as the head of the Maritime Silk Road, which inspired his Belt and Road Initiative, and which forms the origin of the province's fame in producing tea, porcelain, and silk. But Xi's connection with Kuliang began on April 8, 1992, when he read the *People's Daily* article, "Ah! Kuliang," about Milton Gardner, an American physics professor at the University of California, Davis, who all of his life longed to return to his idyllic childhood home on Kuliang Mountain.

Kuliang Mountain, 2023

In 1886, foreigners and Chinese enduring the sweltering summers of the "Fuzhou Furnace" were delighted to hear that Baptist missionary Simeon F. Woodin (1833–1896) had rented a house for the summer on Kuliang. A year later, the British

Consulate's doctor, Thomas Rennie (1865–1938), built Kuliang's first Western-style villa. At an altitude of 800 meters and bordering the Min River estuary, Kuliang was usually seven to eight degrees cooler than downtown Fuzhou, and the little community of foreigners and Chinese quickly grew to over 350 homes, as well as stores, athletic facilities, a church, and a post office.

Gail Harris as a girl growing up at Kuliang Mountain in the 1940s, then returning for a 1923 reunion of Americans whose families have lived there through many generations.

On August 21, 1921, Rose Talman, a Reformed Church missionary in Xiamen, described summers on Kuliang in her unpublished memoirs:*

> We entertained at coffees, teas, dinners. Played rook a lot. Men played tennis. There were conferences, trophies, and entertainment during the week.... Families brought

* Rose Talman, "Our China Years 1916-1930," unpublished memoir in the author's private collection.

> down one or two of their own servants to take care of the extra work. Fortunate we were if we had good servants. Because of the inconvenient kitchens (charcoal stove braisers*) our first term, it would have been almost impossible to have done our own cooking for more than a few meals. It was a day-to-day process with no refrigeration upcountry.

Over the years, I've tracked down many Americans who spent childhood summers on Kuliang. Even into their eighties and nineties, they remembered vividly Kuliang summers—especially the romances. John Anderson, who was born in Xiamen in 1939, shared how his British parents met in Kuliang. Peter had studied chemistry in England and taught English in Amoy (Xiamen), and his mother, Constance, was a missionary nurse in Fuzhou. Peter and Constance met on Kuliang in early August 1936, were engaged within two weeks, and married on November 10, 1936, in Fuzhou's picturesque Anglican Stone Church.

A group of girls proudly dubbed "The Jolly Six" at Kuliang in 1924.

---

* We still had charcoal braziers when I moved to Xiamen in 1988.

But no one, foreign or Chinese, was ever more passionate about Kuliang than Dr. Milton Gardner, who taught physics for thirty years at the University of California, Davis. As the 1992 *People's Daily* article read, Gardner's missionary parents, who arrived in China in 1890 or 1891, lived in Fuzhou from 1901 to 1911 and spent ten idyllic summers on the cooler heights of Mount Kuliang.

The Gardners returned to the US in 1911, and Professor Gardner led a rewarding life—he helped MIT develop the radar systems to beat the Japanese and Germans, and taught physics in California and Pakistan—but for the rest of his life his dream was to revisit his childhood Kuliang home.

Milton especially missed Chinese food. He often spoke of his family's Chinese garden, especially its strawberries, and until the end of his life he never went a day without eating a bowl of Chinese rice porridge. If asked to cook, he invariably prepared a Chinese dish.

Sadly, Milton was paralyzed in 1976, just as the normalization of US and China relations would have made a China visit possible. He retired in 1978, and in his remaining years he was often heard murmuring, "Kuliang, Kuliang." His wife shared that even on his deathbed in 1986, Milton murmured, "Kuliang, Kuliang".*

Milton's wife Elizabeth visited China five times, traveling to several provinces in her futile search for Kuliang. But in 1990, as she was rummaging through her husband's China memorabilia, she found eleven Chinese stamps, some of which were postmarked, "Foochow Kuliang." She was delighted when a Chinese student staying in her home explained that "Foochow Kuliang" was Guling, Fuzhou, but in the Fuzhou dialect Milton had spoken as a child.

---

* Liu Zhonghan, "Ah, Kuliang!" *People's Daily*, April 8, 1992.

The Chinese student was so moved by the Gardners' passion for Kuliang that he wrote "Ah! Kuliang!" in April 1992, and as soon as Xi Jinping read it in *People's Daily*, he invited Mrs. Gardner to visit.

On the evening of August 21, 1992, Xi Jinping welcomed Elizabeth at the Fuzhou Hot Spring Hotel, where he shared with her that Fujian had enjoyed centuries of international exchanges and friendships. Marco Polo sailed home from Fujian in 1292, and Fuzhou was the port of departure for Chinese navigator Zheng He (Sanbao), whose seven epic voyages probably inspired the legend of Sinbad.

Elizabeth could not have imagined how meticulously Xi Jinping had prepared for her visit. She was delighted to learn that he had even tracked down nine of her husband's childhood friends—all in their nineties. Elizabeth set off for Kuliang the next morning, video camera in hand, to record for family and friends back home the places and people of her husband's childhood.

One of her first stops in Kuliang was the massive thousand-year-old cedar tree that dominates the settlement. Milton's childhood friends remembered racing the young American like monkeys up the giant evergreen—and Milton's delight on the rare occasions he beat them to the top. A *Fuzhou Daily* reporter snapped off a small twig and gave it to Elizabeth, saying, "Maybe you can feel Milton's joy in this branch." Elizabeth carried that twig the entire day.

When Elizabeth shared some of Milton's old photos of Kuliang, including one of a tiger, a childhood friend recalled how Milton's older brother had joined locals on a tiger-hunting trip. Amoy Tigers, known today as South China Tigers, reached up to nine feet from nose to tail, and had long terrorized

Fujianese. *The Travels of Marco Polo*, compiled over 700 years ago, noted, "In these parts are tigers of great size and strength.... The magnitude of tigers renders travelling through the country dangerous, unless a number of persons go in company."*

Enjoying some free time on a Kuliang afternoon in 1924.

At the end of the day, Elizabeth rested contentedly on a veranda's cane chair, eyes closed, facing the sun. The director of Fuzhou Foreign Affairs, Chu Yanli, said, "I think she was telling her husband she had finally found the Kuliang he had longed for. It was very moving."

Xi Jinping knew that Milton had collected a pair of lacquer vases, so he gave Elizabeth a pair of Fuzhou's famous bodiless lacquer vases. Elizabeth in turn presented Xi with her husband's treasured lacquer vases. Over one-hundred years old, his parents had brought them back to California in 1911 and for almost a century Milton had meticulously coated them every few years with a special preservative. Xi was delighted and promised to

**The Travels of Marco Polo*, original title, *Livres des Merveilles du Monde*, circa 1300.

display them in a Fuzhou museum.

Over the following days, Elizabeth sampled Fuzhou cuisine—[quotation mark facing the wrong way] “Buddha Jumps the Wall” soup, Fuzhou fish balls, guang-bing flatbreads—visited Fuzhou’s panda park, a senior citizen’s activity center, and workshops producing Fuzhou famous crafts such as lacquerware and carvings of shoushan stone, miniature cork carvings of classical Chinese landscapes, and buffalo-horn sculptures.

Although Elizabeth had already visited China five times, she said this trip was the most eye-opening and heart-warming because she finally got to see the places and people of her husband’s Kuliang childhood.

American missionaries living in Kuliang in the early twentieth century stayed in touch with those back home—a fine symbol for the connection between the two countries that continues to this day.

Kuliang Friends

On December 10, 2016, Elyn MacInnis emailed me to say she was setting up a group called Kuliang Friends (which now has over fifty members). It took Elyn a year of research to begin tracking down some of the old Kuliang families, and another half year for her to convince them to visit China in the summer of 2017 when we had our first Kuliang Family Heritage Conference. The families who visited were happy to help rebuild the lost history of Kuliang and share their stories.

Elyn's father-in-law, Donald MacInnis, a missionary in Fuzhou in the 1940s, was a teacher and a coast watcher for the Flying Tigers, the daring group of US volunteer fighter pilots who helped China fight Japanese troops in World War II. MacInnis recorded his experiences in his book, *China Chronicles from a Lost Time: The Min River Journals*. He marveled at China's changes when he revisited Fujian in 2002, and wrote:

> There are no foreign gunboats patrolling China's rivers today. Nor are there special treaty rights, extraterritoriality or concession zones controlled by foreigners. Warlord battles, rampant banditry, and women's bound feet are distant memories. Girls as well as boys have access to universal education. A railroad and a paved highway now run through Shaowu, the river town that could only be reached on foot or by small boat in earlier years. A new generation has no memory of the War of Resistance [Second Sino-Japanese War], the civil war, or the chaotic years of the Cultural Revolution.

After Donald's death, in accordance with his will, Elyn and her husband scattered some of his ashes over the Minjiang

River, Fuzhou's mother river. Elyn not only led the 2023 Kuliang Friends visit but also donated three suitcases full of her China and Kuliang memorabilia to a Kuliang museum. As Elyn told a *Global Times* reporter, "The place where our ancestors lived and left traces is home, and we are sending old objects home this time."

The 2023 Kuliang reunion also included Priscilla Brewster Gill, now in her eighties. She was born in Fujian and lived in China for twelve years. Her father, Harold Brewster, was also born in Fujian, and was fluent in the Fuzhou and Putian dialects. A Methodist medical missionary, he ran a Kuliang clinic and was the last foreign president of the Union Hospital (today, the Fuzhou Medical University Union Hospital). When the Japanese occupied Fuzhou and shot anyone violating their ban on Min River travel or transport of medicines, Dr. Brewster risked his life by continuing to transport supplies by boat between hospitals.

Priscilla recalled how she helped her father take care of patients, and how when she injured herself, villagers tended to her wounds. "We were like family," she said. "China is the hometown where my heart belongs."* No wonder Dr. Gardner longed for the people of Kuliang.

People-to-People

Xi Jinping has long said that people-to-people exchanges are an important bridge between nations. In February 2012, when Xi was vice president, he shared the Kuliang story at a luncheon in the US with over seven hundred Chinese and US political and business figures and added that there were many more touching stories like this between the American and Chinese peoples.

* "Kuliang story of China-U.S. friendship passed down for generations," *The Los Angeles Post*, July 17, 2023.

When Xi met with Bill Gates in Beijing on June 16, 2023, Xi said, "The foundation of China-US relations lies in the people. We have always placed our hope on the American people and wish all the best for the friendship between the two peoples."

As I noted in the preface, Chinese like to say, "Alike, but different." Fortunately, as this book's stories show, what unites us—love of family and country, and hopes for a peaceful, prosperous future for our children—far outweighs what divides us. May we not only build upon our common ground but also learn to accept and even embrace our differences.

We hope you enjoy this book's stories of friendship—and that you will share your own.

CHAPTER TWO

Don MacInnis

A Flying Tiger's Love for China

In Xi Jinping's 2023 letter to Friends of Kuliang, he mentioned Don MacInnis' love of China, which began in the 1940s when he taught in a remote school in Yangkou, Fujian. Outraged by Japan's brutal aggression, Don returned to the US and after intense training returned to China to help the Flying Tigers defend China. After the war, he returned to China with his wife and son to again teach in Fujian, where his second son was born. Although the family had to leave Fujian again because of the complicated relationship between China and the US, he fully expected to return.

In 1974, he joined the US-China Peoples Friendship Association (USCPFA) and in 2004, in his eighties, returned as a volunteer to the Fujian school where he had taught in the 1940s. On his deathbed in 2005, his lap was filled with cards and notes that he had been reading from his students and friends in China. But what gave Don, and two generations of his descendants, such a passion for the Chinese?

In 1980, an interviewer asked Don if he had been interested in China as a youth. He said, "No. I can't remember a thing. I never even thought of China!"*

The Chinese Flying Tigers

* Donald MacInnis, "Midwest China Oral History Interviews" (1980). *China Oral Histories,* Book 56, http://digitalcommons.luthersem.edu/china_histories/56.

Ironically, it was a visit to Japan that led Don to China.

"We are a nation of patriotic and peace-loving people!" the Japanese speaker said at Tokyo's 1940 seventh Japan-America Student Conference. But Don and many of the other fifty-seven American students had their doubts.

James Halsema, a twenty-one-year-old Duke University student, wrote in his diary that even though the "academic conference" supposedly aimed to "promote mutual understanding, trust and friendship," every lecture aimed to "convince us of the rightness of their cause, the strength of their patriotism, and their dislike for war."*

The fifty-eight American students were followed everywhere by four teams of security: male Japanese students, regular local police, the Gestapo-like military police, and Foreign Ministry officials. Police watched from every street corner as the Japanese photographed the Americans bowing in front of such tourist spots as the imperial palace, but the Americans were not allowed to take their own photos.

One Japanese official complained that the Chinese were anti-Japan; he did not mention, of course, the two-hundred-thousand Chinese murdered by Japanese during the Nanjing Massacre three years earlier. And the US, he claimed, had been preparing for war with Japan for two decades. Thus, his thinking went, the peace-loving Japanese had been forced by China and the US to prepare full plans to control East Asia as an outlet for their excess population and to secure resources.

Ironically, he also argued, "the US should loan money to

---

* James Halsema, 1940 *Japan-America Student Conference Diary, Publications of the Center for East Asian Studies, University of Kansas, Electronic Series,* Number 1, Center for East Asian Studies.

Japan to develop a new China." Don MacInnis was soon to see Japan's plan for a "new China."

In 1940, Sidney Chen, a graduate of the University of Southern California and dean of Fujian's Anglo-Chinese College, spent the night at the MacInnis home, and surprised young Don, at that time a student at the University of California, Los Angeles, by saying, "Why don't you come to China some day and teach English?"

Don MacInnis understood the aggression of China's neighbor early on, as he related in his book *China Chronicles from a Lost Time*.

Don mumbled, “Ok,” and promptly forgot about it until a few months later when he was preparing to attend the conference in Japan. Don sent Chen an airmail letter to see if he was serious about teaching in China. Don recalled spending twenty-five cents on the airmail stamp—”a lot of money in those days”—when his jobs paid only twenty-five cents per hour. His big investment seemed wasted, as he did not hear back from Chen. But after the conference, and tours of Korea and Manchuria, Don returned to Tokyo to find a letter from his father saying that Chen had replied. His dad had also included a check for $200, adding, “If you want to go to China, it’s ok with me.”

That $200 investment changed the MacInnis family’s path for three generations.

Don took a Japanese ship to Shanghai, spending three days and nights on crowded straw mats with Japanese packed in the belly of the ship. In Shanghai, he learned that Fujian’s Anglo-Chinese College had moved from coastal Fuzhou to an interior mountainous area. He was astonished to hear firsthand of Japan’s ruthless bombings across the country (evidently part of their “new China” strategy). The conference in Japan had really convinced him and others that Japan had no thoughts of war, at least with the US. But Don wrote in *China Chronicles**:

> I saw the bombed-out sections of Shanghai, the ragged hordes of displaced Chinese, the Japanese troops, their tanks parked just outside the International Settlement and their warships anchored in the Huangpu River. The

---

* Donald MacInnis, *China Chronicles from a Lost Time: The Min River Journals* (Eastbridge Books, 2009).

> Japanese, I was told, had attacked China without warning or reason, had repeatedly bombed innocent civilians, and had fought their way into all the northern provinces, all the coastal provinces from Hebei to Guangdong, and all the Yangtze River cities as far up as the Three Gorges. They had committed atrocities in Nanking and elsewhere. They controlled all the seaports, all the major manufacturing centers, and all the major railroads.

For Americans back home, it was still "business as usual," and the US continued to export oil and iron to Japan even as it ravaged China. But Americans back home and Americans in Shanghai were furious. Don wrote:

> They knew how cruel and vicious the Japanese soldiers had been in their treatment of Chinese civilians: bombing, terrorism, and raping, and so on. Shanghai had been just viciously bombed several times. Obviously, the Japanese knew they were not bombing military targets. This was years before the WWII bombing of civilian targets, so this was considered to be very savage and uncivilized for them to bomb civilian residential areas in Shanghai.

Don noted that China, however, was increasingly "viewed by Americans as the great, heroic nation of Chinese people resisting the brutal Japanese aggression. And it was true, too.... Certainly it was that experience that marked my life, I suppose, more than anything else because the year in China was where I developed enormous love and empathy for the Chinese people."

But Don was distressed by foreigners' attitudes and lifestyle as Chinese struggled just to survive. Don told his interviewer that war-torn China had millions of suffering refugees, but China's ports "were still privileged zones for foreigners. . . .The Chinese were simply there to provide services for the foreigners." It was no different when he reached Fuzhou, where he observed, "The foreigners had their clubhouse, their big mansions on the hill. They had their servants and their extraterritorial privileges, while the millions of Chinese around them struggled to survive. That all made a great impact on me. It was a contrast between the privileged life of the foreigners, including myself. Even though I did live at the same level as my Chinese colleagues up in the village, I still knew that it was just an interlude in my life. I had my American passport and could always cable home to my father for money."

Smuggled to Fujian

Don tried to book a ship to Fujian but discovered that Japanese had blockaded the coast and mined the harbors, so he smuggled himself into Fujian on one of the rusty old boats running up and down the coast illegally with cargo and passengers. "I shipped out on the *Ariadne Moller*, which was a small coastal vessel that was just loaded from the bottom of the hold to the top deck with refugees—Chinese who were trying to get from Shanghai to Foochow [Fuzhou]."

"The captain of our ship," Don said, "was a grizzled old British ex-patriate who had been up and down the China coast all his life, I guess. The crew was Chinese. It was a real rust bucket—coal burning."

Of the seven hundred or so passengers, only four were foreigners, including Don, a young White Russian girl, and a missionary-architect named Paul Wiant who had lived in Fuzhou since 1917 and worked with the Fujian Construction Bureau. The fourth foreigner was Dr. Robert McClure, a Canadian smuggling two hundred or three hundred crates of medical supplies to Fuzhou's Christian Union Hospital.

As soon as the ship left Shanghai harbor, waves from a typhoon—still far from the coast of Shanghai—tossed it like a toy. All seven hundred passengers cowered below deck until the captain finally anchored near some small islands to wait out the storm. "The typhoon just whipped us for three days and nights. It was just terrible. The captain told us later he gave up—he thought we were going to be lost. He thought the ship was going under. Several of the Chinese died and were thrown over the side."

Three days later they set out again but were forced again to seek a safe harbor. This time, however, they encountered a Japanese navy destroyer. Japanese officers boarded the ship and ordered the captain to return to Shanghai. As the ship headed back north, a Japanese plane flew overhead to make sure it had turned around. But that night was a full moon and pitch dark, so to avoid having to refund the passengers, the captain dropped off all passengers except McClure and the White Russian girl at a Fuding estuary. Don said he should have stayed on the ship, because McClure did not want to unload all of his medicines, so the captain turned the ship around again and took McClure and the White Russian girl to Fuzhou. Don, however, had to hike seven days to get there. Fortunately for Don, he met a passenger named Paul Han Ding who spoke English and was returning to Fuzhou, where he taught at Fujian Christian University. Don tagged along with Paul and his two teenage female cousins.

Don told his 1980 interviewer:

The next day we started walking up and down all the hills and the valleys. It was beautiful country, very mountainous. Seven days and nights. I got a terrible case of dysentery; it just laid me out. They finally got a sedan chair for me because I had to be carried. I had no energy; I lost thirty pounds in seven days." Don noted later that he never did return to normal weight until after he left China. Once in Fuzhou, he had to be hospitalized for a few days and then rest until he had the strength to make the trip upriver on a big flat raft with a small cabin and a wood-burning steam engine. From Nanping, he took a bamboo raft that was poled up the river for a day or two.

Once I got to Yangkou, I spent a year there in a village completely cut off from the outside world, really. No highway, no trains, no airplanes—nothing. The only way to get out was by boat, what we called rice-boats.

In spite of Yangkou's remoteness, the Japanese bombed it on occasion, but people took it in stride. Don said, "They never bothered us." As soon as the air raid alarms went off, everyone scrambled to a countryside graveyard, and as the hated Japanese bombers roared overhead, Don and the other foreigners stood with the Chinese and shook their fists at the enemy. "The war brought everyone together," Don said. "Of course, it was fascinating to be a part of this school, in a refugee location. All of this energy and sense of resolve to survive under very difficult circumstances. And to resist the Japanese invader."

But other schools near remote Yangkou were less fortunate. American missionary Francis Wilkinson wrote to her family:

"On Easter Tuesday (April 23, 1941) at 11:00 p.m. we were

bombed—very accurately and from an enormous height. We couldn't even see the planes. Fifty bombs—mostly near us. Five of our [school] boys, one school coolie, and the school doctor and his wife and little girl were killed.... We have heard that Foochow [Fuzhou] fell on Monday."*

Don's school's move to Yangkou was only temporary—or so they had hoped. They used any kind of public building they could get, including old Buddhist temples or guild halls (similar to labor unions). Don's small dorm room was in a temporary building with mud walls and wooden floors. But though accommodations were spartan, he liked Chinese food—though he never had enough to be full. They ate mainly rice and vegetables, and tiny bits of meat, fish, or tofu. He supplemented this sparse diet by having a local use his hand-operated stone mill to grind peanuts into peanut butter. Local Chinese wondered why on earth he bothered grinding them. Even with peanut butter in his diet, he was still twenty-pounds underweight when he left China.

As Yangkou's only American male, and the only young westerner, Don was very popular. He filled his after-class hours with the Chinese playing volleyball and basketball, hiking in the countryside, or putting on plays such as Dicken's *A Christmas Carol*, which he rewrote in simpler English. He even held an American square dance.

Don also enjoyed simply learning about Chinese people's daily lives. "For me," Don said, "it was a learning experience just to go down the street, watching the blacksmith, or the cooper making wooden barrels and buckets, or the furniture maker, shoemaker and tinsmith."

---

* MacInnis, *China Chronicles*.

One of Don's big regrets was he did not pick up the language, but the school wanted him to teach English, not learn Chinese. He never imagined he'd soon have a year's intensive military language training.

After teaching for a year, Don went back down river to Fuzhou. After making his way through the line of Chinese guerilla forces surrounding the Japanese lines, the Chinese guerillas snuck Don through the Japanese lines on a rice boat smuggling what seemed to him to be a few million rifle cartridges.

Don MacInnis with two granddaughters

It was weeks before Don and twenty-five other foreigners caught a ride on an empty Japanese troop ship to Taiwan. Fuzhou had just endured the bubonic plague, so the Japanese sprayed them head to toe with insecticide to kill fleas. In Taiwan, their bags were put through a disinfectant gas chamber, and they were all interrogated. Don said, "We were all very careful not to say anything that would help them. At least, we thought we were."

Don finally reached Shanghai but did not have enough money for a ship home, so he waited at the American consulate each morning for two weeks until an American captain came in looking for someone willing to work for their fare. After reaching home in the middle of November 1941, a Wisconsin radio station asked Don if he thought Japan would go to war with the US. In spite of all that Don had seen, he said, "Oh, no, there's no chance of any war with Japan." When Japan bombed Pearl Harbor only three weeks later, Don noted the Japanese had used "the oil and iron bought from the US."*

The bombing of Pearl Harbor made Don more determined than ever to return to China. He joined the military as soon as he graduated from UCLA in the summer of 1942. "I enlisted in the Air Force because I wanted to get back to China. I knew the Air Force was the only American service in China—the Flying Tigers." After basic training he was sent to the University of Chicago for a full year's intensive Chinese language study. Don said, "It was a wonderful school. The army invented the whole new method of teaching which they still use today." Sixty percent dropped out of the program, unable to cope with eight hours of Chinese, five days a week, "but those who stuck it out spoke Chinese fairly well by the end of the year."

Don MacInnis

After language school, Don was recruited by the Office of Strategic Services, the forerunner of the CIA. After six weeks of training, he was flown over the Himalayas into West China's Kunming, then sent on a special mission to Fujian because of his knowledge of the province. He was flown over Japanese lines, dropped off in an area controlled by Chinese guerillas, and then made his way to a base near Jiangxi Province. After getting his radio and jeep, he drove across Fujian to Zhangzhou, across from Xiamen, and spent the last six months of the war in Fujian.

Don told his 1980 interviewer, "I masqueraded as a weather officer. I used that as a cover. You can't go around saying that you're doing intelligence. Even the Chinese whom I met believed

* China Oral Interview, 1980.

I was a weather officer." Don traveled with Chinese guerillas and collected information on the Japanese to send to the military. The Chinese were heartened by the US sending two bombers each day from the Philippines to bomb Japanese retreating from Xiamen down the coast to Swatow.

Don said the Chinese dreamed of defeating Japan and going back to normal life:

> After all, they had had eight years of enormous disruption and enormous suffering. They all looked forward to getting back to a normal life again and restoring the momentum of building a modern China, which had been interrupted in 1937 by the Japanese attack. Of course, the big difference between '37 and '45 was the fact of the Kuomintang government of Chiang Kai-shek was no longer as effective or as honest or as respected as it had been. Inflation, the disintegration of the economy had already begun earlier and it got worse through the years that followed.

After the war, Don was sent to Xiamen, and then spent three days getting to an airfield in West Fujian's Changting, where he waited three days for a plane to fly him to Kunming. After another wait, he was flown to India, where he waited several weeks to get on a ship home.

Don had married Helen just before going overseas and he was anxious to spend Christmas with her. He made it home on Christmas Eve. After a month's leave, Don was discharged from the service, and the couple drove to California for Don to join a graduate school at Stanford. Don recalled that he wasn't sure what he wanted to do with his life—except return to China.

From March 1946 to the end of summer 1947, Don worked on a Stanford graduate program in international studies, with a focus on China, finishing everything but his research thesis, "Food and Nutrition of the Chinese Peasant," which he planned to finish in China. He almost joined a United Nation's food and relief program for China but they would not allow him to bring his wife, so he returned to Fuzhou to teach at Fukien Christian University in 1948. But perhaps it was just as well. Don told the 1980 interviewer:

> In Foochow [Fuzhou], UNRRA [United Nations Relief and Rehabilitation Administration] people were primarily Europeans instead of Americans. They had a bad reputation. By that I mean that they were paid high salaries and weren't doing anything. Also, the program they were operating was very sloppy and very corrupt. And a lot of the materials they were supposed to be giving to the poor people were not getting to the poor people. It was being siphoned off into the black market.

Don was surprised to learn of the extent of China's Civil War—and amazed he'd been sent to Fuzhou with a seven-months-pregnant wife and a one-year-old son but given no briefing, training, or preparation. He wrote, "We might have gone out without even knowing there was a civil war on, except that I'd already been in China and I knew there was."

The school was in chaos. Many of the seven-hundred students were frustrated by the nationalist government's incompetence and corruption, and increasingly sympathized with the Communists—though not openly. "The nationalist government could be brutal with pro-Communist students."

The economy was also falling to pieces. Don said, "While we were there, the Chinese dollar went completely bankrupt so that they had to issue a new currency." The "gold yuan" was worth four yuan to one US dollar, but it rapidly dropped in value to twenty to one, then fifty to one, and finally to one thousand to one. "Within less than a year, I believe, this had gone bankrupt, so it was worthless.... China was just falling apart."

But foreigners, by and large, were insulated from the chaos. Most of them continued to live in large homes behind high walls, with small armies of servants to care for the buildings and gardens. Don said "It was all very colonial." Some foreigners did balk at the excess. Muriel (Caldwell) Pilley, who was born in Fuzhou in 1907 and raised in China, insisted her agency build her a smaller house. But as Don wryly noted, "They were still inside the compound for Americans only."

The MacInnis family, however, lived in university housing, "on the same scale as our Chinese colleagues.... And the student dormitories were right there, right next door. We were living in the midst of the Chinese community."

Don's second son, Peter, was born in Fuzhou's Kuliang in 1948, but as uncertainly increased, the US Embassy recommended Americans leave China. As Don said, "The US Embassy cannot tell you what to do. They can only recommend." But eventually families with small children were asked to leave at least temporarily. "We had a baby that was just a year old, and our other son was two and a half," Don said, "We had no choice, we had to leave."

In May 1949, the family boarded a ship from Fuzhou's Pagoda Anchorage to Hong Kong, and after a long wait caught a plane to Los Angeles. They left behind in Fujian their trunks with wedding presents, fully expecting to return soon. Don never imagined that, because of US and China tensions, he'd not return to his beloved Fujian and the Yangkou school for over fifty years.

Over the decades, Don dreamed of returning to mainland China. When interviewed in 1980, Don explained, "I think that my early impressions of the Chinese people were of a people who were enduring undeserved suffering and deprivation . . . . That was reinforced by the post-war years when things were falling apart."

"There's some kind of mysterious love for the Chinese people, or affection, that takes place in almost anybody who goes out there," Don said. "The Japanese had brutally invaded China. Yet the Chinese people and the foreign friends who were there helping were carrying on life in a very vigorous fashion, despite the Japanese."

In 1988, eight years after Don's interview, his son Peter moved with his wife and two daughters to China, where they would become two of the mainland's few permanent resident foreigners—and the Flying Tiger's two granddaughters would grow up on Chinese TV and be loved by millions as the "strange white Chinese girls."

CHAPTER THREE

Charlotte MacInnis (*Ai Hua*)

Granddaughter of Kuliang Flying Tiger

When Chinese students saw Charlotte MacInnis on the University of Arizona's Tucson campus, a lot of them would say, "Wow! What are you doing in the US?"

They were surprised at seeing this American girl in America because, for over two decades, millions of Chinese had watched Charlotte and her sister grow up on China Central Television (CCTV), China's national television network.

Charlotte's Chinese stage-name is *Ai Hua* ("To Love China")—which certainly fits. She and her sister, Mika, have both gone so far as to claim China as their first home and the US as their second. Charlotte is so fluent in both the Chinese language and culture that many Chinese believe she must have at least one Chinese parent. But her love for China is not surprising given that she is a third-generation American lover of China. Her grandfather was the

Flying Tiger Don MacInnis. Her father, Peter, was born in Fuzhou on Kuliang in 1948 when his parents taught at Fukien Christian University (FCU). Peter spent his first summer on Kuliang, living in the same house that had belonged to the Gardner family.

In 2017, after spending most of her life in China, Ai Hua accepted a position at the University of Arizona's Confucius Institute (which closed in 2020). The Chinese were delighted. If anyone could help Americans better understand China, it would be Ai Hua, who had grown up in China.

Zhao Chen, director of the UA Confucius Institute—who moved to the US in 1988, the same year that Ai Hua and her family moved to China—told *This Is Tucson,* "It's not just the language. The language is something you can learn in class, but the culture—how to behave and talk to people—it just blew you away. If you closed your eyes, you wouldn't know she was an American girl speaking . . . . She knows both cultures, so she can easily translate one culture to another, and people notice that. It's so smooth."*

Chinese at the University of Arizona were delighted when Charlotte co-hosted two of the institute's Spring Festival Galas—but she was in her element after two decades of wowing Chinese audiences on CCTV.

Third-Generation China Lovers

In 1988, the same year that I moved to Xiamen with my wife and small sons, the MacInnis family moved from West Hartford, Connecticut, to Nanjing, which in ancient China means

* Johanna Willett, "You've Probably Never Heard of This UA Employee, But She's Super Famous in China," *This is Tucson,* March 23, 2019, https://thisistucson.com/tucsonlife/youve-probably-never-heard-of-this-ua-employee-but-shes-super-famous-in-china/article_e2e80a44-4763-11e9-bcba-8f35e3baa6fb.html.

"Southern Capital." Even into the 1990s, foreigners were still a novelty in China—especially young ones like Charlotte and her sister Mika, ages seven and nine, respectively. Wherever they went, they got what nineteenth century foreigners called the "China Stare." Charlotte was quick to point out, however, that Chinese were not unfriendly—merely curious. Many Chinese who had never seen a foreigner assumed they were a Chinese minority—perhaps ethnic Russians from North China.

Infant Peter MacInnis is napping in this 1940s photo from Kuliang.

Although foreigners were a novelty to Chinese, the MacInnis girls were very familiar with China. They had grown up listening to tales of China from their grandfather and their China-born father. No one was overly surprised when Peter announced he wanted the family to move to Mainland China. And after settling in Nanjing in 1988, it was his wife Elyn's passion for Chinese culture, as well as her involvement in numerous social projects, that helped give the sisters such a love for China. Elyn wrote in one of her books, "Although my family did not have deep roots in China (I was born in New York City!), I felt curiously at home in Nanjing. What I remember was the kindness of our friends and co-workers, who gave us great happiness."*

After a few months of Chinese tutoring at home, the girls began spending mornings in a classroom with Chinese children and afternoons at home studying an American curriculum. Charlotte recalls that Chinese schools were a challenge at first. She was not used to sitting at a desk, silent and unmoving until called upon by the teacher, but everyone else did it, so it eventually became second nature.

Charlotte recalled her first day of school was a freezing day in February and she wore several layers of clothing on top of overalls. When during a break she asked to go to the restroom, the teacher asked a Chinese student to show her the way. To her surprise, over thirty girl classmates followed her to the toilet and stood watching as she entered the doorless stall. Privacy is a luxury in a land of one billion people, and when she could not get them to leave, she slowly began to disrobe, layer by layer, as the girls watched. She recalled, "They probably wondered why I had to take off all of my clothes just to go to the toilet!" After removing a couple layers, Ai Hua lost her courage, put her sweater back on, and said to the crowd, "Never mind. I don't need to go now!"

Scrambled American Eggs

Chinese in the West are often called "bananas"—yellow on the outside, white on the inside. The MacInnis girls were called "eggs": white on the outside, yellow on the inside. But rather than feel at ease in both cultures, they felt out of place with both

---

* Elyn MacInnis, *Character Reflections: Contemplating the Spiritual Wisdom in Chinese Characters* (Createspace Independent Publishing Platform, 2011), 4.

Chinese and foreigners. Charlotte told a *China Daily* reporter in 2011, "No matter how Chinese I feel or how perfect my Chinese is, people will look at me and say, 'You are not Chinese.' And when I go back to the US I am regarded as strange."

The girls did not know the latest American slang, fashions or fads, or the most popular songs and movies. They were poster-child "Third Culture Kids" (TCK)—children who spend their formative years in a culture different from that of their parents. TCKs' rich, diverse experiences and bilingualism often give them greater confidence. In the US, eighty-one percent of TCKs obtain a bachelor's degree, compared to only twenty-one percent of non-TCKs. But being ill at ease in both home and host cultures can complicate adapting to adult life.

Fortunately for Charlotte and Mika, they had a China-born TCK father and a very insightful and encouraging mother had studied Chinese at Harvard and quickly adapted to life in China.

The young MacInnis family in the late 1980s in Nanjing.

Charlotte said to *This Is Tucson,* "So I'm really, really grateful to my parents for maintaining my open outlook on things—through my entire life here and growing up."

The girls' parents ensured they embraced Chinese culture without forgetting their American roots. There were no international schools in Nanjing at that time, so they attended classes with Chinese children in the morning and in the afternoons were homeschooled with American correspondence programs, supplemented by a library of English books they'd brought from home. Elyn and Peter also involved their daughters in helping society.

In addition to teaching Chinese at middle and high school levels, Elyn worked closely with hospitals, programs for special needs students at the Xuzhou Pengcheng Special Education School, or the Golden Key educational program for blind children in rural areas. Elyn also made the contact that led to their daughters' TV careers.

In 1995, the family moved to Beijing and the girls caught the nation's attention when they emceed the China TV Drama Flying Awards, China's oldest award for TV dramas.

Although both girls were fluent in Chinese, Charlotte claims they were chosen not because of their skill but because, at that time, Nanjing had few foreign adults and even fewer foreign children. "They had no one to choose from—just my family, and my sister, and I!"

Charlotte told *This Is Tucson's* Johanna Willett that her older sister, Mika, was clearly the better of the two. "My sister was this delicate, graceful willowy young girl, and I was more of a tomboy and not as graceful at that age. . . ."

But the Chinese were delighted by their performance. During the program, the girls met children in the famous Little Red

Flower Art Troupe. Elyn MacInnis was never one to miss a good learning opportunity for her daughters. So, she boldly asked the troupe leader, "Can you teach my girls to sing Chinese songs?"

Charlotte and Mika not only learned to dance but also to sing different forms of Chinese opera, including Henan Province's *Hua Mulan Opera*, traditional songs such as the popular "Jasmine Flower" (茉莉花), and the comic dialogue which won the hearts of millions—and scores of TV invitations.

The girls' home province was Jiangsu, so they adopted the stage names of *Ai Jiang* and *Ai Su* ("Love Jiang, Love Su). But in 1993, when they performed at a Spring Festival Gala for five provinces, they changed the name of their comic dialogue from *Ai Jiangsu* to *Ai Hua Dong* ("To Love East China"), and their own stage names to *Ai Hua* (Love China) and *Ai Dong* (Love East). When they were performing for CCTV later, the director said, "How can you be called "To Love East China" on national TV? Just change your name to *Ai Beijing—Ai Bei* and *Ai Jing*. But the girls themselves insisted on being *Ai Zhonghua* ("To Love China"). So Mika became *Ai Zhong* and Charlotte *Ai Hua*.

Being so much in the limelight might have gone to their heads had the girls' parents not brought them back down to earth each summer by spending summers in the US, where they were no different from other children around them. Mika said that in the US, "We didn't have that feeling of, 'oh my goodness, you're so special.' It was more like, you had to work hard and put time and effort into what you're doing, because if you're not doing it well, we'll pick somebody else."*

In 1997, Charlotte landed her first recurring role, co-hosting over one hundred episodes over three years of CCTV1's *Laughing*

* Willett, "You've Probably Never Heard."

Teahouse, a short segment that was part of a famous Chinese weekly program called *Zheng Da Zong Yi*.

Charlotte attended Chinese school until her senior year in China. Her final year was at the International School of Beijing to boost her English in preparation for college. While attending the International School, Charlotte had classmates from all over the world, including a young American named Josh Hannum, who had also grown up in China and whom she would marry.

When Charlotte's teacher learned that a Chinese college they were visiting had prepared a welcome performance, she hastily threw together a selection of performances for the college. Charlotte had no idea what would happen when she agreed to sing a Chinese song. As soon as she began speaking in Chinese, the college students recognized her, and her foreign classmates wondered why on earth she was so popular.

In 1998, Charlotte returned to the US and received a BA in drama and dramatics/theater arts at Columbia University, where her grandmother had earned her PhD in psychology. But when she returned to Beijing in 2002 to start a professional career in entertainment, she faced unexpected challenges. Although her colleagues and friends were Chinese, and her mastery of the language and culture had improved, it was hard finding roles for a foreign woman. Perhaps she was not that surprised. After all, Hollywood was still using white people to play Chinese—and other Asian—characters.

Charlotte did not want to play the typical "ignorant foreigner role." She told *This Is Tucson,* "I didn't spend my whole life in China to end up playing that role." As a result, she landed only small parts on TV shows such as *Evidence* (穿越激情) or movies such as *The Earth Dances* (大地起舞) or *Passion* (穿越激情).

Charlotte's most memorable role, however, was in Jackie

Chan's *Chinese Zodiac* (茉莉花). She said of Chan, "He is the same on camera as he is in real life. He learns everybody's name—from the guy who takes out the trash on set to the lead actress."

Interestingly, her husband Josh also had a touch of stardom. In 2010, he starred in the comedy *Once Upon a Time in Tibet,* which was adapted from the novel *Cats of Shambala* by the novelist Tashi Dawa.

The MacInnis family was awarded for their multiple generations of being friends of China.

Given the lack of acting roles, Charlotte accepted more invitations to host live events and TV shows, but the more she learned about China's culture, and the more questions she heard from both Chinese and Americans about the differences between China and the US, the more she wondered if there might not be better ways to help bridge the gap between East and West. In 2017, at age thirty-six, she decided to tackle the great divide from the

American side—and a Confucius Institute in the US seemed a good place to start.

In 2004, China joined a long tradition of state-sponsored cross-cultural education and language programs. China's network of Confucius Institutes has been compared to France's *Alliance Française*, which was formed in 1883 and today promotes France's culture and French as a second language in over eight hundred centers in 137 countries. Italy's Dante Alighieri Society, formed in 1889, is now in over sixty countries. Portugal created its Instituto Camões in 1924, and the United Kingdom's British Council, founded in 1934, is in over one hundred countries.

China was relatively late in starting such an organization, opening its first Confucius Institute in Seoul, Korea in 2004, and its second at the University of Maryland. Today, the world has hundreds of Confucius Institutes, including over one hundred in the European Union alone.

Charlotte MacInnis is now the Assistant Dean for Curricular Affairs & Operations for the university's global microcampuses and other international education programs. She joined the University of Arizona's international office in 2017 and was previously the senior director for China and East Asia Programs.

And Charlotte's husband, Josh, who spent twenty-eight years on Mainland China, is President and CEO of the Arizona School of Acupuncture and Oriental Medicine. The school's website notes of Josh, "He offers the school a unique cultural bridge between Chinese and international circles, and US culture."

Well said. Both Josh and Ai Hua are indeed unique cultural bridges between the US and China, and perhaps someday we'll see a fourth generation follow in their footsteps.

CHAPTER FOUR

How Richard Sears Became Uncle Hanzi

I wasn't surprised when Richard Sears whipped out his pad and pen during a dinner in Beijing to explain a Chinese character's origin. If he'd seen a large enough bone in the soup bowl, he could have duplicated the three-thousand-year-old oracle bone from which the character originated.

Over the past two decades, this white-haired, bearded American, known throughout China as "Hanzi Shushu" (汉字叔叔, "Chinese Character Uncle"), has spent his entire life savings of some $300,000 to single-handedly build a database of over a hundred thousand ancient Chinese and modern characters that even Chinese scholars refer to.

But what gave an American from a small Oregon town such a passion for Chinese characters?

In 1972, the year that President Nixon visited China, Richard was a twenty-two-year-old physics student at Portland State University when he decided to see the world and learn a foreign language. He was on his way to Africa, not Asia, when he learned that the most foreign language for English speakers was Chinese, which is spoken by far more people than English is, and is one of the few languages that still uses ancient script. So, he set his heart on learning Chinese. As Richard told a *Beijing Review* reporter, "The most important thing in one's life is to find an interest and pursue it, which usually means taking a risk."*

Richard took the risk by buying a one-way ticket to Taiwan.

Richard did not speak a word of Chinese when he landed in Taiwan with only a few dollars in his pocket and "the idea that I would become fluent and literate in Chinese." Although he did pick up spoken Chinese fairly quickly, he discovered why Chinese is considered the world's hardest written language to master. The language is so intimidating in part because Chinese and foreigners alike usually rely upon rote memorization, but unlike English with its twenty-six-letter alphabet, Chinese has tens of thousands of characters, with a minimum of two to three thousand needed for basic daily use. Richard said, "I found that almost all Chinese had learned to read and write by absolute blind memorization and almost no one had a clue where the characters actually came from. . . . I do not like to blindly memorize stuff without understanding why."

After two years in Taiwan, where he supported himself by teaching English, Richard returned to the US to finish his bachelor's in nuclear physics and master's in computer science. He then worked as a researcher at a US government lab and later as a software engineer at several Silicon Valley companies. But although he had picked up spoken Chinese, eighteen years later,

---

* Li Qing, "US physicist devotes his life to telling the stories behind the transformation of the Chinese script," *Beijing Review,* May 6, 2021 https://www.bjreview.com/Lifestyle/202104/t20210429_800245179.html.

at age forty, he still could not read Chinese. As Richard shared on his website, Chinese Etymology, "I was still faced with the prospect of learning to write about five thousand characters and sixty-thousand-character combinations. The characters were complex with many strokes and almost no apparent logic."

If only Chinese characters were as logical and recognizable as the ancient pictographs from which they originated.

Ancient cave art is found all over the world, from the 64,000-year-old Neanderthal red hand stencils in Spain to a 40,000-year-old pig hunting painting in Indonesia and the 28,000-year-old charcoal drawings in Australian caves. Yet in nowhere but China did these prehistoric pictographs evolve into a writing system that is used to this day. By the time of China's first emperor, Qin Shi Huang (221–207 BCE), the nation had numerous writing styles. Fortunately for Chinese civilization, however, Qin Shi Huang not only unified China, built the Great Wall, and standardized weights and measures, but also unified diverse writing styles into a standard script that helped improve education and administration. The Han Dynasty (202 BCE–CE 220) then created the official *lishu* script, as well as the faster "cursive" grass script. The Eastern Han Dynasty's (25 CE–220 CE) *kaishu* script, with its simple but elegant vertical and horizontal strokes, became the foundation for characters used for almost two thousand years until China simplified writing to help reduce illiteracy from eighty percent in 1949 to less than ten percent in 2020.

But few modern Chinese characters bear any resemblance to what they represent. Although today we can still recognize the pig in forty-thousand-year-old Indonesian cave art, it takes a good imagination to see a fish in 鱼—and I'd go bananas trying to decipher 苹果 as an apple. It's no wonder that Richard rebelled at rote memorization of characters like *guàn* 罐 (jug, can) or *cuàn*

竄 (flee), and decided to see if he could make learning easier, faster, perhaps even fun, by bringing to life the stories of characters' origins and evolution. For example, it is easier to write the eighteen-stroke *cuàn* when you remember it is composed of a *xué* (穴, "hole") above a *shǔ* (鼠, "mouse"): a mouse flees into its mouse hole.

As Richard explored characters' origins, he was intrigued to find many errors in the two-thousand-year-old *Explanatory Dictionary* (*Shuōwén Jiězì*,说文解字) compiled by philologist Xu Shen (許慎, 58 CE–148 CE). Xu Shen did not create China's first dictionary but he was first to make characters easier to look up by arranging them according to components called "radicals" (*bùshǒu* 部首), organized from simplest (一, *yī*, "one") to the most complex (龠, *yuè*, "flute"). Xu Shen was also one of the first to research and explain characters' origins, though he made errors because the oracle bones and bronzeware scripts, ancient even in his day, had yet to be unearthed.

In 1990, faced with so many inaccuracies and misunderstandings of ancient characters, Richard decided to compile a database to help "separate good opinions from bad ones." But he did not act on his idea until four years later when he was chatting with friends in Taiwan and suddenly collapsed. "It was very sudden," he said. "I was able to run a marathon the year before, so I didn't expect a heart attack." He was even more surprised when he returned to the US for surgery and was told he had a year to live.

Richard said, "If I knew I had only twenty-four hours left, what would I do? All I could do is call my friends and say goodbye. But if I had a year left? I decided to computerize *Shuōwén Jiězì*."

Richard scanned every character of *Shuōwén Jiězì*, then scanned 96,000 characters from three other ancient books. And after compiling the world's most extensive database of ancient

Chinese characters, Richard began exploring how they evolved from ancient pictographs—a task he found was endless. "You never stop asking questions," he said. "It keeps getting deeper and deeper.... Every part of every Chinese character is derived from a pictograph. If you know the original pictograph and the original logic, you can trace the evolution of every character and thus every Chinese character becomes logical. If you don't know these origins, you are just trying to memorize a bunch of complicated strokes."

In 2002, after seven years of scanning every ancient character he could turn up, Richard launched a self-supported, advertisement-free website showing the origins of Chinese characters and how to pronounce them in Mandarin Chinese and dialects such as Cantonese. But after spending some $300,000 of his life savings on the website, he lost his well-paying Silicon Valley job due to a downturn in the economy. Undaunted, he worked several years as a night watchman so he could rest by day and learn Chinese characters by night. He said, "I didn't earn much, but at least I had time to read Chinese books."

In 2003, Richard took a job as an engineer for the Tennessee Valley Authority and continued to work on his website. Yet even as the world's most extensive database of Chinese character origins, for a decade the site received only eleven thousand to fifteen thousand hits a day and donations of less than $100 per year. But that changed overnight, in 2011, after a Chinese Weibo blogger recommended Chinese Etymology. Visits soared to over six hundred thousand a day and Richard received over three thousand emails in one week. Overnight, Chinese netizens began calling Richard *Hanzi Shushu* ("Uncle Hanzi"). "I like the nickname," Richard said. "I've been studying Chinese characters since I was forty. Thinking of the money and energy spent, most people thought I was crazy. Now finally people think it's worthwhile."*

Encouraged by Chinese enthusiasm, Richard moved to China to devote the rest of his life to researching Chinese, but had to leave his small one-room apartment a year later when his tourist visa expired. Fortunately, Dixin Yan, a user of his website, shared Uncle Hanzi's plight on Weibo. Yan wrote, "He's given everything to Hanzi . . . down-and-out. . . . He hopes to find a regular job as an English teacher or translator, so as to continue his life and research on Hanzi in China. Please forward this post!"

The message was forwarded over forty thousand times, bringing Richard donations and many job opportunities, including five interviews in Beijing.

A decade later, Richard is still on a crusade to help both Chinese and foreigners escape the dispiriting trap of rote memorization by bringing Chinese characters' stories to life. He worked with a Nanjing firm to create animated "Chinese Character Origin" cards that show the evolution from oracle bone pictographs to modern characters. That project led to Richard receiving Nanjing's 2020 Jinling Friendship Award.

Richard has also brought Chinese characters to life for children by appearing on CCTV's *First Class for New Semester,* which is aired before each academic year for primary and secondary schoolchildren.

But the highlight of Richard's time in China was receiving permanent residence in 2020. Visa woes finally behind him, Hanzi Shushu told a Xinhua reporter, "Finally, after many years, I have permanent residence in China, so I plan to stay here for

---

* Wang Linyan, "A Man of Character," *China Daily*, last updated November 16, 2021, https://global.chinadaily.com.cn/a/202111/16/WS6192f7c1a310cdd39bc75807_2.html.

the rest of my life. China is my home."

Today, Chinese Etymology receives about three-hundred thousand visits per month—half of them from China. One surprised Chinese student posted online, "Unexpectedly, the Chinese character website that I often visit was created by an American".

Richard Sears

Uncle Hanzi's website explains the origins of not only over a hundred thousand ancient character forms but also fifteen thousand modern characters. "You can put in any simplified character or any traditional character. And you can see the change over 3,500 years," Richard says. "And you can see the logic explained."

Richard has learned the logic behind the characters not just from books but also by studying ancient Chinese technology, which helped him see how four hundred characters arose from spinning and weaving alone. And visits to the countryside to observe farmers' lives and work have helped him understand the story behind such characters as "home" (家, *jiā*), which is a roof (*mián*, 宀) over a pig (*zhū*, 猪). In flood-prone South China, many houses were built on stilts and pigs lived beneath the house. Chinese and foreigners alike appreciate that Richard's site is not only exhaustive but also very user-friendly. A Chinese student specializing in Chinese characters posted online, "Previously, to trace the evolution of a Chinese character, I had to dig it out from piles of books. But since I came to know the Chinese Etymology site, all it takes is a click to display the oracle, bronze, and seal characters."

Not all comments are positive, however. One netizen said, "Isn't this just a website made by an old foreign man? What's the point? It cannot make much money."

But Chinese netizens jumped to his defense, with one reminding readers that the $300,000 Richard spent on the site "was made before 2002, and all used on the website for basically zero return. And that was all Uncle Hanzi had. It's much more than just a website. Respect to Uncle Hanzi!"

Another Chinese called Hanzi Shushu "the contemporary foolish old man who moved the Mountain! Kudos to his dedication over the decades. I think he deserves a special allowance for his tremendous contribution to Chinese characters."

It is clear that Hanzi Shushu's goal for decades has been not profit but a better grasp of what he calls the "miracle of Chinese characters." "I will always try to study and figure out things that we don't understand about the origins of Chinese characters. We understand a lot, but we don't understand everything," Richard said. "My philosophy is *huo dao lao, xue dao lao* (活到老学到老; "learn as long as you live")—so never stop learning."

CHAPTER FIVE

Julian Quander's Second Chance in China

"Do you believe in second chances? Well, I do!" Julian Quander (*jiékù*,杰酷) wrote in Master Translations's 2022 Home Away From Home essay contest. "In 2010, I was blessed with an opportunity of a lifetime that would change my life forever."*

This singer, actor, and model's life-changing second chance was China, where he became the first African American in the country to start a record label—and he makes music that inspires others to keep dreaming. As Julian told Popular Hustle, "My music is for that kid with a big dream, that person with a broken heart, or that person who wants to stay positive and happy. I

---

* Luz M. Sanchis, "18. Do You Believe in Second Chances? Julian Squander," Master Translations, June 10, 2022, https://www.mts-tech.com/2022/06/10/18-do-you-believe-in-second-chances-julian-quander/.

believe my purpose is to uplift others with my music because, at the end of the day, it's about y'all."*

But Julian himself is from a long line of dreamers. The story of the Quanders, one of the oldest documented African American families in the US, has been told in the United States and other countries through books, media, an Emmy-winning TV special and Smithsonian Museum exhibits. Julian's ancestors include Amkwando, who was captured in present-day Ghana and brought to Maryland as a slave before 1684, and Nancy Carter Quander, one of George Washington's slaves who was freed in 1801 at the age of thirteen.†‡ By the end of the American Revolution, forty percent of Fairfax County—where George Washington's Mount Vernon estate is located—were enslaved. But today, Fairfax County has a Quander School, and many Quander roads and streets in the DC area, including a Quander Street facing the Washington Navy Yard.

Although the Quander family endured centuries of slavery, they also produced four US Army generals—three of whom were West Point graduates—and leaders such as the DC judge, Rohulamin Quander, who wrote the family's history, and concluded that African Americans deserved "to hold our heads just as high as other communities. Indeed, we too shared in

---

* "There's a Beast in the Far East by the Name of Julian Quander," *Popular Hustle*, July 3, 2023, https://www.popularhustle.com/theres-a-beast-in-the-far-east-by-the-name-of-julian-quander/.

† Interview with Rohulamin Quander, July 1985, in *Telling Histories: A Collection of Transcribed Interviews of Quander Family Members . . .*, ed. Rohulamin Quander (Quander Historical Society, 1998), 1:3–8.

‡ "Washington's Slave List, June 1799," Founders Online, National Archives, https://founders.archives.gov/documents/Washington/06-04-02-0405.

the building of this great nation and in seeking to fulfill the American Dream."

Julian Quander has very big shoes to fill.

Julian Quander

Although born the youngest of three sons in Washington, DC, Julian grew up in Maryland, and as with many children, it was a teacher that helped Julian find his life's passion. When he was seven, his third-grade teacher, Mr. Smith, asked the class for volunteers to audition for the Montgomery County Youth Chorus. Julian was the only one who dared raise his hand. As he told *Muzique Magazine*, "I believe this may have been the first audition in my life. He took me to the piano and we did some basic scales and sang some simple songs. He told me I passed and

I was in the choir. That's sort of when the music bug started."*

That "music bug" became Julian's life. As he told *Vents Magazine* decades later, music is "harmony, melody, love, expression, every emotion you can feel, instrumentation, all these different things just piled up that create this frequency which we really can't explain. We can try to explain it on paper through notes and lyrics, but it's quite a mystery at the end of the day just like our universe."†

But "music in college was tough," Julian said. He majored in classical voice and jazz vocal performance, and the more he learned, the tougher it got. "It's a lot of work and just like any other field, the discipline has to be there. It was difficult. It kept on getting harder and harder each year, but the most beautiful part along the way is the camaraderie with your teachers. Especially your vocal teachers. My vocal teachers left an everlasting impression on me. The breathing techniques, the confidence, leading a band, posture, and connection. All these elements have to be trained into you. It's not an overnight journey. It takes a long time to get good and you never stop learning."

Julian's passion and persistence paid off. He landed first place in the National Association of Teachers of Singing competition (NATS) and in 2009 won the Cab Calloway Vocal Competition in Baltimore, Maryland. With these successes under his belt, Julian was hoping for experiences to travel and perform live, but

---

* "Julian Quander Interview with Muzique Magazine," *Muzique Magazine*, July 8, 2023, https://muziquemagazine.com/julian-quander-interview-with-muzique-magazine/.

† Deny Smith, "Into the Mind of Passionate and Creative Music Artist Julian Quander," *Vents Magazine*, July 4, 2023, https://ventsmagazine.com/2023/07/04/into-the-mind-of-passionate-and-creative-music-artist-julian-quander/.

he never imagined his future lay on the other side of the planet.

In 2010, Julian was asked to sign a four-month contract as lead singer for Deluxe, a band playing in Shanghai's new five-star Park Hyatt hotel. Julian's family could not believe it and his friends were skeptical—until he showed them the plane ticket.

"When I arrived in China, the entire vibe was new and intriguing," Julian said. "I felt captivated by the new experience and I enjoyed it. All alone in such a big city meeting new band members and awesome people, while doing what I loved, which was singing."

Julian Quander on stage

The four-month Park Hyatt contract ended, but not Julian's newfound love for China. He stayed in Shanghai for three-and-a-half years, but then he "hit a roadblock. I had to take a break and recharge. I had trouble figuring out a real suitable plan that could benefit me to have a long-term future in China. I'll admit; I was putting loads of stress on myself, so I gave up.... Can you believe it? I gave up and left China and went back home."

Julian returned home in defeat. "I felt as though I had left such a great place and a part of me was left behind. I had such a big dream for China.... I decided to compose and write a music album about my experience called *Shanghai to DC*."

While in DC, Julian kept contact with his friends in China, and in 2015, an entrepreneur he'd known in Shanghai named Kevin Ke (柯桦龙) wrote to him about the beautiful island city of Xiamen where he had just started Skeyou (三蝌优网络), a multinational advertising and public relations company with offices in Shanghai, Beijing, and Paris. "It's such a peaceful city. Warm weather, wonderful people, great food and plenty of opportunity. I think you would love it here."

It was perfect timing. Julian had just completed a new album, and when he suggested to Kevin a big tour of Xiamen and other cities in China, his friend said, "Let's do it!"

Julian fell for Xiamen as soon as he disembarked the plane and saw the sun sparkling on the beautiful blue waters around the island. Julian wrote, "Have you ever closed your eyes and dreamed about living on an island filled with an abundance of seafood, tropical fruits, clear blue skies, kind people, and peacefulness? Well, that was the total vibe I got when I came to Xiamen, China for the first time. It felt like home, and till this day, it's been my home. This city is special, and the community around us is loving."

This time around, Julian was determined to make the most of his "second chance." He was better prepared and focused and had a plan of action. "I'm going to live more in the moment, enjoy the experience more, learn the culture, and the language."

But Julian quickly found that success as a musician in a foreign country "takes a lot of patience and time to be heard, especially if you're doing your own music." He kicked off his 2015 *Shanghai to DC* tour at the Xiamen Exhibition Center, which led to opportunities to perform in cities across China. In 2017, Julian and friends captivated Xiamen people across the entire island with "flash mob" performances of his song, "QQ Tang," with accompanying dance. Many Chinese had never heard of flash mobs and had no idea what to make of them—but they caught on quickly, and many delighted onlookers joined the dance.

Many Chinese had never heard music like Julian's, which is no surprise. He has created his own genre. Julian said, "I would describe my music as somewhere between soul, R&B, and pop: soul pop & B. There we go. I got my genre now y'all. I think in this day and age we need more positive music. Can we take a break from all the violence and cursing in music? My music is clean. You aren't going to get any X-rated stuff out of me. That's just not who I am."*

In 2017, Julian registered in Xiamen JQ Nation, his own cultural media/record label which he had created back in 2010. He was excited about starting China's first record label by an African American, but he admits "it was a big step. I never went to business school. I just jumped into it without any kind of experience whatsoever. This was a challenge because it involved a lot of different things, but luckily I had the right team in place to guide me through the process."

When Deny Smith of Vents Magazine asked how he stays grounded while juggling so many things, Julian replied, "To be honest, I'm trying to figure that out. It can be overwhelming being an artist, and entrepreneur all at once. I have a great team, and I found that sometimes it's okay to give responsibilities to others you trust and can get things done."

---

*"The Quandary of Julian Quander," July 4, 2023, Hustle Informer, https://hustleinformer.com/the-quandary-of-julian-quander/.

Julian and team proved they were up to the challenges, and, as Xiamen and China grew, so did Julian's vision. "Over the years," he said, "I've seen the city of Xiamen grow tremendously. A lot of new opportunities and ventures are constantly happening. New housing developments, shopping malls, restaurants, the new Xiamen University campus, and even an entire metro system. I encourage Americans and other foreigners to visit Xiamen and see the amazing things firsthand. The growth is amazing to witness and as the city of Xiamen grows, we must also grow along with it."

On July 8, 2017, Julian performed at Xiamen's ceremony for Gulangyu Island's designation as a UNESCO World Heritage Site. He was as proud of his city's achievement as the four million other Xiamenese, and in 2018 he put his feelings for Xiamen and China into his "dream project"—a song called "I Love China."

"This fun-loving tune gets to the core of how awesome this place really is," Julian said. "And till this day, I still perform it at every event I take part in." After the song landed media attention across the country, *Xiamen Daily* asked Julian to create an "I Love Xiamen" version. "We did just that. That project became quite successful and to this day is still a hit."

Julian has of course experienced his share of challenges in China. He had to learn a language and culture very different from those back home, and how to do business in China. But he's determined not to squander his second chance in China.

Julian said, "I believe my biggest challenge was dealing with myself. Staying motivated and energized is never an easy task. As foreigners, we may at times think things may need to be done a certain way, but we have to remember we are in a foreign country, and our ways are not always the same. I believe being a foreigner in China takes a lot of patience. First, we need to learn the basics of the language, and secondly, find our place within the fast-moving pace of China. There is a place for everyone here, but it's our responsibility to seek it out. I believe we need to have respect, kindness and not feel so overwhelmed with things."

Learning Language through Song

Julian's friends are not surprised he learned Chinese through music—or that the motivation for it was a girl. Julian told Kwadwo Sampany-Kessie, founder of the YouTube Elementary Chinese channel, that when he found he could not communicate with a Chinese girl that he liked, he thought to himself, "I'm a singer. I can't communicate with her. I got to do something."* So, he wrote her a song. But Julian admitted, "This was a long time ago, and it was the worst Chinese song ever. It was my first time ever writing a Chinese song. And it made no sense. It was horrible. But she understood. And I never got a date. You know what I mean?"

Kwadwo laughed. "So, you failed?"

"Yes, I failed." But that "horrible song" helped motivate him to put his heart into learning Chinese. Julian now says that learning Chinese is like diving into a swimming pool. "You got to really dive in and, almost like being an actor, you got to act Chinese, you got to act like you're playing a script, you're playing a new role because when you do a new language, have fun with it. It's so much fun, learning Chinese. It really is. Every day is like an adventure. Every day I learn something new. Oh, that's what that means. Oh, oh, oh really? Okay."

When asked his most useful Chinese phrase, Julian replied without hesitation, "'Everyone should have a dream.' *Měige*

---

* "Learn Chinese Through Songs? How to Learn Chinese—Julian Quander," Elementary Chinese channel, YouTube, August 28, 2017.

rén dōu yīnggāi yǒu mèngxiǎng (每个人都应该有梦想). It's a great conversation starter."

Julian's latest project is an imaginative music video called "Never Let the Love Stop," which is a reminder to both himself and others to never give up on one's dream. Julian set the video in his "Asiaverse" and "JQ University" because it kind of focuses on the Asian experience. Many people don't know anything about this side of the world, and I hope to bridge the gap between the USA and China and continue to inspire more foreign artists to come to Xiamen, China and display their talent.

"I encourage people to be international. See the world. Live life and get your butt out of bed and travel. China is a special place and will always remain in my heart forever. I believe in second chances because I am living proof of one."

CHAPTER SIX

China Forever for Badminton Becky

"I never had any special draw towards China," Becky admits, but when she realized she could teach English there—making money to put toward her true passion, traveling—she moved to China "for a six-month lark." That was in 2009 and she hasn't left since. Becky shared on her website, "Something about the culture and the people attracted me in ways my home country never did. . . . There's too much misunderstanding between the West and China, and I hope to bring a unique perspective and hopefully a bit of understanding to it all."*

But her passion for China was certainly not love at first sight. In fact, she wanted to flee home to the US after her first morning in Hangzhou. She would have never imagined that China would become home—and that she would become known in China and abroad as "Badminton Becky."

---

* "About Me," About, BeckyAnces.net, http://www.beckyances.net/about/, accessed May 7, 2025.

Badminton fans watching Becky spring up and down the court find it hard to believe that "Badminton Becky" (Becky Ances, *Lóng Xiǎobīng*, 龙小冰) had never played any sports until she was forty. In college, doctors warned her that any sports could endanger her life because of a genetic blood vessel disorder in her intestines. But Becky didn't mind skipping sports. "I grew up a wallflower/art kid, going to art school and hating anything physical and thought jocks were dumb," she said.

Her "art kid" mentality was not surprising, given that her quaint hometown of Peterborough, New Hampshire, population 6,000, is famous for nourishing artistic communities such as the famous MacDowell artists' colony. And in 1883, Peterborough opened the nation's first tax-supported library, with the postmaster doubling as the librarian. This charming town was also known as the world capital of magazine production (per capita), and to this day, one third of its residents embrace entrepreneurship from the comfort of their homes or thrive working remotely.

But while other Peterborough residents found inventive ways to work from home, "fragile" Becky had a profound passion for something entirely different: travel.

A wanderlust soul, Becky visited over thirty countries and even drove across America twice. She would have happily spent the rest of her life on the road, but her life took a dramatic turn in August 2009, when, in her quest to travel and make money for more travel, she agreed to teach for six months in China's Hangzhou. It was only supposed to be a one-semester trip to save up money while experiencing a new culture.

Becky was confident she was prepared for "crowds, cars, chaos, etc.," having survived a ten-day tour of China the year before. But by noon of her first day in Hangzhou's Lin'an District, she felt overwhelmed. "I chided myself for being such an idiot and wondering how I could get back to America as fast as possible." *

Marco Polo wrote of Hangzhou, his favorite Chinese city, "It is without a doubt the finest and most splendid city in the world." To this day, Chinese still quote Marco Polo, "Heaven above, Hangzhou and Suzhou below." But Becky's first impression of Hangzhou was not heavenly.

On day one, with a few hours free before meeting her new boss, Becky set out to explore the shops and restaurants near campus. Even just after dawn, Hangzhou was already hot and humid, and "art girl" Becky, who hated jocks and sweat, was soaked in sweat within minutes.

The Chinese school was neat and clean inside, but the city outside the school gate resembled a movie about the apocalypse. "This is what I have to look forward to for six months?" she asked herself.

There was no sidewalk, so she walked down the side of the dusty road. Giant trucks loaded with rocks and rubble roared past so close that it seemed like a game of chicken in which they vied to see who could come closest to a pedestrian without actually hitting them.

Becky later discovered the chaos was part of a renovation project, and within a few years the entire area had nicely paved roads, modern buildings and beautifully landscaped grounds. But on day one, Becky thought this was the norm for Hangzhou.

It took Becky half an hour to finally realize she had taken a wrong turn and was headed away from the city center instead of

---

* Luz M. Sanchis, "Home Away From Home: Becky from The United States #12," Master Translations, July 7, 2021, https://www.mts-tech.com/2021/07/07/home-away-from-home-stories-from-expats-in-china-12/.

towards it. Frustrated, she turned tail and headed back down the dusty road towards her school. She was thirsty, and her throat was scratchy from swallowing dust kicked up by trucks, but she could not speak a word of Chinese, so she didn't dare enter the tiny shops. She said:

> I just kept walking, hoping I would make it to my new apartment before passing out of dehydration. "When I finally made it home after about an hour (though it felt like an eternity), I guzzled a jug of water and cleaned the dust from my face, promising myself that I would never leave my house without an escort and translator. In all the months of preparing myself for China, I never once imagined I'd find myself in a situation like I just had. I had been excited, nervous about this new adventure, curious about what it would be like, but never scared. Not until that first day. As I was wiping dust from my face, I chided myself for being such an idiot and wondering how I could get back to America as fast as possible.

In spite of her especially bad start, Becky told Boston University Radio (WBUR) that she was shocked at how quickly she came to love life in China:

> My life in China seemed downright normal. All my friends back home assume I am having some exotic adventure everyday but actually I wake up, drink tea, go to work, eat lunch, see my friends, play on the internet, play badminton, have dinner parties with my friends and stuff like that. The biggest difference is I speak another language while doing much of these things (and eat Chinese food

> when I go out), but daily life here is much more normal than people might expect.

She decided to stay for an entire year, and then another. "And now, I've given up on saying one more year. It's basically forever now. Now my family is, like, 'Are you ever coming back?' And I'm like, 'Hmm. I don't know.'"

Becky with her coach, Chinese badminton legend Lin Ze Xiong.

Three to Six Months to Live?

It wasn't all fun and games, though, and the real world eventually came crashing down on her China life. Four years after moving to China, just as Becky was becoming fluent in Chinese and making more friends, she experienced severe abdominal pain. The diagnosis was shocking: "You have stage IV liver cancer.... You have three to six months to live," the doctors told her. "We'll need to do some more tests to see if there's treatment available, but the hospital is all full right now. So, you'll have to come back Wednesday."

Becky recalled how she went home, alone, and spent three days trying to come to grips with having only three to six months to live. "If this was true, I was obviously going to quit my job immediately, and have a wonderful last three to six months."

Further tests revealed she did not have cancer, but the vascular disorder she'd been diagnosed with thirteen years earlier was spreading and showed no signs of stopping. She was spared an immediate death sentence, but the disease would inevitably shorten her life.

"It definitely changes your life," she said about her disease. "It definitely changes everything that comes after it.... You have to do what you want to do, and you can't waste time."*

At thirty-nine, Becky moved from Hangzhou to Xiamen. Becky quickly made many friends, though most were foreigners, mainly Europeans. Her friends loved badminton and invited her to join them on Tuesday and Thursday nights, but the artsy sports-averse Becky politely declined. But when they planned

* Kevin Ferguson, "'Badminton Becky Moves to China...And Discovers Her Love for a Sport," WBUR, December 1, 2017, https://www.wbur.org/onlyagame/2017/12/01/badminton-becky-ances-china.

a friend's surprise birthday after a game on badminton night, Becky decided she would join them in playing badminton.

Not Love at First Smash

Like many Americans, Becky had no idea that badminton was a real sport, but as *Yuánfèn* ("fate") would have it, she had ended up not only in one of the most famous countries for the sport, but also the most famous city. The Chinese national badminton team is the most successful badminton team in history, and Xiamen is home to many of the nation's top players, including several who rank number one worldwide. The "God of Badminton," Lin Dan, the greatest player in badminton history, is from just west of Xiamen.

But badminton, like life in Hangzhou, was not love at first site. She had no sports equipment or clothes, so she wore khaki pants, sneakers, and a cotton shirt that was soon heavy with sweat and uncomfortable to move around in. Becky hated sweating, hated running, and hated that her feet hurt. Even worse, the windows were all closed to avoid wind disrupting the shuttle, and there were of course no air conditioners. When she asked her friends if the indoor badminton court got hot in the summer, they laughed. "Oh, yeah, really hot! And it really smells bad!"

Becky decided she'd play until the summer but then stop because, "I hate sweating. I hate smelly people." Besides, her doctor's order to "not play sports" was always in the back of her mind.

But as the weather heated up, and badminton got sweatier and smellier, Becky kept playing—first once a week, and then twice. Even for Becky, it was hard to admit a new passion was growing within her, but she could not deny that this sport was stirring something within her, and badminton nights became her favorite nights of the week. She decided to take her newfound passion as far as she could, and asked twenty-year veteran, Lin

Ze Xiong to be her coach, "and before I knew it, I was obsessed, playing and training as much as I could."*

Ironically, Becky had taken up badminton to spend more time with her foreign friends, but she began skipping parties for the badminton courts. She even left the foreigner's badminton group, since it was just for casual play, and joined more competitive Chinese groups to improve.

"Xiao Bing's biggest advantage," her coach said, "is she is persistent, earnest, and never gives up. These are the most important and irreplaceable qualities that all athletes must have to become a master hand. She is very committed to her goal. A lot of people give up when facing obstacles. But not Xiao Bing."

The girl who disliked sports and jocks began to play in amateur tournaments, interview top professional players, produce a YouTube channel about China badminton, and in 2018 began running a badminton training camp in Xiamen. But her competitive days were numbered.

Sports a Killer?

Doctors had warned Becky over a decade earlier that sports could kill her, and after a few years of playing badminton, the disease reared its head again. She had to stop her intense training and reduce playing from four nights a week to two. Even so, it only dampened her abilities, not her spirit. No longer able to move and play as fast as the others, Becky lost her competitive edge, but her appreciation of badminton deepened, and she now plays just for the sheer love of the sport. Win or lose, she sees every night of badminton as a gift. She knows she might not physically be able

---

* "About Me," Badminton Becky, http://www.badmintonbecky.com/sample-page/, accessed May 7, 2025.

to play forever, so she is grateful for every moment, regardless of how she plays. She promised herself she would follow her passions and, sick or healthy, she has done just that. Becky said that being sick "has definitely helped me be braver in life . . . and just, kind of, go for what I want to go for."

Xiamen Fangirl

Some still wonder if Becky will ever return to the US, but as she has said, "Anyone who knows me knows I am a total Xiamen fangirl. I love this city and I love the person I've become while living here. The city is an island, and it has mountains literally next to the ocean. It's small both in population and in actual size so it has a cozier feel than other cities in China. Also, due to the small size, the expat community is much more integrated. There's no expat bubble here and all the activities organized by expats are half in English, half in Chinese. Most foreigners here can speak at least basic Chinese. And there are always activities like weekend hikes, beach parties, book clubs, craft fairs, and lecture series. Xiamen people come up with unique and interesting things to keep everyone busy."

And Badminton still keeps Becky busy.

Becky's Chinese Badminton Summer Camps

Becky has found that not only are there big cultural differences between the US and China but also that their perceptions of badminton are very different. She found that while Xiamen has over sixty public badminton halls and dozens of private ones, there are few in the US, with the closest to her parents' home almost an hour away. She said, "It's no wonder Americans don't play badminton much because they just aren't exposed to it like other sports."

Americans see badminton as an outdoor/picnic kid's game, and not as the intense indoor game which has set Guinness World Records as the fastest racket sport in the world. A smash by Malaysia's Tan Boon Heong was clocked at 493 km/h (306 mph). Tennis, by comparison, has been clocked at the relatively sleepy speed of 263.4 mph. So Becky has determined to spread the word and show Americans how intense, and rewarding, badminton actually is.

Badminton has been a vehicle for Becky to be an ambassador and a passionate advocate for sport and cross-cultural understanding.

Becky challenged an American who had played badminton when he was younger. He claimed to be good. "All right, let's go play," she said. After five minutes of warm up, the American was sweating and out of breath. "Let's take a break," he said, gasping.

"Uh, we're not playing yet. We're just warming up," Becky said laughing. The American agreed that competitive badminton was far more intense than he had expected.

Uniquely positioned as an American badminton player in

China, with a growing fan base watching her weekly videos, Becky decided to start badminton summer camps for foreigners who did not speak Chinese. "I know a lot of foreigners want the experience of learning badminton in China because of the high level of skill here, but with the language difference it is tough, and finding information on the internet in English isn't easy. So, I started these badminton camps just to help people come to China to train."* Becky not only arranges the hotels, transportation, and training, but also makes sure to mix in a rest day for touring Xiamen and experiencing a bit of Chinese culture.

Becky said, "Badminton changed my life completely . . . . I also have a lot of confidence in other parts of my life because of my success in badminton. When you see yourself grow and improve in one part of your life, like me with badminton, you realize you can change and improve other parts of your life the same way!"

Becky is not exaggerating when she says badminton changed her life completely. She even met her Taiwanese partner of seven years on the badminton courts.

"So now, it's China, forever," Becky says. "And badminton, everything."

---

* Lorraine Lam and TSE Bun, "Badminton Becky: The Story of an American Girl Learning Badminton in China," Badminton Professor, September 26, 2020, https://badmintonprofessor.com/interviewing-badminton-becky/.

CHAPTER SEVEN

Tennessee Caldwells

Naturalists and Tiger Hunters

"Two things in Fukien impressed Marco Polo: the beauty of the women and the size of its tigers."

Mackenzie-Grieve, Averil, A Race of Green Ginger, *Putnam, London, 1959*

When Gail Harris visited Kuliang in the summer of 2023, she said in Fuzhou dialect, "I'm home!" Seventy years seemed to vanish as she clasped hands with childhood friend, Li Yiying, and reminisced about summers in Kuliang in the 1940s.

Both sets of Gail's grandparents came to China at the turn of the twentieth century. One grandfather, Harry Russell Caldwell, a Methodist missionary and educator in Fujian from 1900 to

1944, built 108 buildings for schools, hospitals, and churches. But the Caldwell family's lasting legacy is their pioneering research on Fujian's ecology, the collection of thousands of specimens for Western museums, their book *South China Birds*, one of the earliest scientific works on China's bird species—and their world-famous tiger-hunting.

Before moving to China, Harry was a successful businessman, outstanding baseball player, avid outdoorsman, and he married the Chattanooga Beauty Queen of 1898. A self-made success like Harry would have never imagined he'd completely fail in China.

As soon as Harry arrived in Fuzhou, he tackled the language like everything else in his life—head-on. But he was so fixated on mastering the dialect that he lost weight, fell deathly ill, and finally returned to Tennessee, tailed tucked between his legs.

Harry lost all interest in China, even refusing to write to friends back in Fujian. And to his dismay, his health continued to deteriorate. The turnaround came when he finally vowed to give China a second try. His health began improving and within a few weeks the family returned to Fuzhou. But this time around, a wiser and older friend suggested Harry seek a more balanced life and find a healthy hobby—and Fujian was just what the doctor ordered.

Back home in Tennessee, the Caldwells had enjoyed exploring the rolling green hills as they hunted, fished, trapped, mined for gold, and explored nature. But after sacrificing his hobbies and interests to move to Fujian, Harry discovered, to his delight, that Fujian was China's most forested province, with endless mountains like those of Tennessee and a biological diversity rivaling that of Eden.

Over the decades, the Caldwells collected so many thousands

of specimens for Western museums that "*caldwelli*" and was included in the Latin names for such diverse creatures as the *Spinibarbus caldwelli* (a carp), *Gonodactylellus caldwelli* (blue-lined mantis shrimp), *Vanmanenia caldwelli* (ray-finned fish), *Babina caldwelli* (frog), and *Stobaera caldwelli* (planthopper).

Harry's son, John, author of *China Coast Family*, was seven when he earned money for the first time by helping a British scientist collect grasshoppers, bugs, lizards, and snakes. John found a grasshopper in Kuliang that was identical to one species in the southwestern United States, suggesting an ancient connection between Asia and North America.

The Caldwells discovered that Fujian is famous for snakes such as cobras, bamboo vipers, and the world's longest snake, the reticulated python (a 32.8-foot python was caught in 1912—though probably not by seven-year-old John).

Young John helped his father write a small paper-bound book called *Birds of the Lower Min Valley*, and when John was seventeen, they published *South China Birds*, compiled from Harry's thirty years of notes. John recalled, "It was truly a family enterprise. Father and I did the research and writing; Morris [John's brother] was the photographer; and Muriel [John's sister] wrote the stories and legends and added color and flavor to its pages." One of the most popular books on Chinese birds for decades, it helped encourage Chinese universities and colleges to engage in research and offer natural history courses. They also compiled a beautiful book about China butterflies, but it would have been too expensive to print a color book.

Roy Chapman Andrews, the "Indiana Jones" who discovered in China's Gobi Desert the first dinosaur eggs and became the American Museum of Natural History's director, made the Caldwell home his base of operations while exploring Fujian.

Andrews, who believed humanity originated in Asia, not Africa, invited Harry to accompany him on his famous three-month Mongolian expedition.

Please—No More Eggs!

One spring, young John was allowed to skip class to help find rare bird eggs for a museum in Cleveland. To find as many eggs as quickly as possible, he posted in a Pingtan Island marketplace that the Caldwells would pay for rare bird eggs if the collector also explained where they were found.

They expected eggs of rare birds from remote islands and beaches, but to their surprise, it seemed every farmer and fishermen had quit work to hunt eggs. They were sold so many eggs, many of them quite common and useless, that they piled them in the courtyard. Still the eggs kept coming, and because it was so hot and humid, many hatched, and chicks of every description ran about the courtyard chirping day and night.

Desperate, they posted another notice: "The Foreign Teachers thank the people of Haitang for their cooperation in bringing many interesting eggs. But please no more eggs."

In his spare time between missionary and naturalist pursuits, Harry Caldwell was also responsible for building schools, hospitals, and churches—doing much of the labor himself. But Chinese most appreciated the Caldwells' courage in the face of the man-eating Amoy Tiger (South China tiger).

Smiling Tigers

The Amoy dialect has many tiger proverbs such as "smiling tiger" (someone who grins even as they plan to double cross you) because tigers are universally feared—and with good reason. Amoy tigers, which reached nine feet from nose to tail, not only waylaid people on trails but dragged them from their homes. One tiger boldly entered a mission hospital near Xiamen at night and hauled off a bedridden patient. They found the tiger's lair next morning and were dismayed to find bloody handprints all over the cave's walls. Like a cat with a mouse, the tiger had toyed with its victim before devouring her.

Tiger Police

Tiger terror did have a bright side: it helped deter crime. As the *China Review* reported in 1896:

> Tigers of enormous size constantly roam about the countryside in the interior, and keep the people in a perpetual state of terror. Not unfrequently they carry off a man, woman, or child, while at work in the fields, of whom nothing more is ever seen, excepting occasionally a few bones. However, they are in one way beneficial to the country, as they effectually prevent all robbers, and night prowlers, from roving about after dark.*

Tiger Truce?

Some villagers believed their local tigers were special because they seldom devoured locals, only outsiders. The reality, of course, was that locals never traipsed about alone at night, whereas outsiders knew no better. When outsiders were in short supply, the tigers again feasted on local folks.

---

* "Amoy General Geographical Description, &c." *China Review*,22, 3, 1896.

Tiger Hunting—Amoy's Noble Sport?

Given Amoy tigers' legendary fearlessness, it's no surprise that H. R. Bruce wrote in "Sport in Amoy," a column in the *China Review*:

> But the crowning sport with which the name of Amoy is associated is the pursuit of that king of the jungle, the wily tiger. Tigers abound more or less all along the coast of China . . . . All Amoy tigers are village prowlers, and man-eaters . . . . It is by no means an uncommon occurrence for a tiger to take a man out of his bed.*

A 400-pound Fukien tiger

Although Bruce called tiger hunting "a noble sport well worth our most ardent devotion," the real heroes were not European hunters but Chinese peasants who were paid a pittance to enter a tiger's lair with a torch on a bamboo pole and flush out the beast for the great Western warriors to shoot.

* H.R. Bruce, "Sport in Amoy," *China Review* 22, 5 (1897).

But the most famous tiger hunters, the Caldwells, put themselves in danger to hunt the tigers that terrorized Chinese villagers.

Caldwell Tiger Hunting

The Caldwells killed forty-eight tigers over their half-century in China, but it was more necessity than sport. After all, the Caldwells delighted in Fujian's rich natural diversity, and the most magnificent creature was certainly the tiger. But they did not hesitate to hunt tigers that terrorized villagers.

One of Harry's descendants told me they regret that Amoy tigers are now found only in West Fujian's Meihua Mountain reserve. But one of my Xiamen University students, whose aunt was devoured by a tiger not far from Xiamen in the 1960s, is grateful tigers now have their own home—and with a reserve spanning 220 square km, they've plenty of room to roam.

Caldwell's First Tiger and The British Consul

Caldwell's world-famous tiger-hunting career began after a Chinese magistrate told him a devilish beast had killed over 250 people. Caldwell asked, "But what kind of monster is this killer? The villagers talk of a saber-toothed tiger who attacks and disappears again with the speed of light. Some swear it is not flesh and blood but a phantom beast begotten of the devils."*

Two nights later, villagers were sitting at the table smoking, a young boy asleep beside them, when something flew into the room. The candle was knocked over, plunging the room into darkness, and the table flew into the courtyard. They relit the candle, and the child was gone.

---

* John Caldwell, *China Coast Family* (Henry Regnery Company, 1953), 38.

Men working fields or walking trails either vanished entirely or were found half-eaten. Crops failed as villagers paralyzed by fear refused to venture outside. Caldwell had no idea what to think, but finally decided that only a tiger could be so ferocious. But when he asked the Fuzhou British consul's opinion, he scoffed: "A tiger in Fujian? Only a missionary could dream up such a notion!"

Caldwell bit his tongue and asked for the consul's help and advice in hunting down the creature that had killed hundreds. The consul replied, "Reverend, I don't think you'd know the difference between a tiger and a civet cat if you met them both side by side."

The Caldwells killed forty-eight tigers over half a century to help protect the community.

While the British consul delighted in telling everyone about the crazy missionary, Caldwell stalked the hills until he finally came face-to-face with tigers—but he missed every shot he fired. Chinese said his rifle was no match for tiger magic, and he himself was perplexed, because he was an expert marksman. But Harry persisted because he wanted the British consul to eat his words. He finally discovered that his Chinese host had misaligned the rifle's sight when he dropped it on a stone. Sight realigned, Caldwell finally shot his first tiger, and thousands of Chinese trailed behind him as he hauled the giant cat on a pole to show the scoffing British consul.

The consul was awestruck, saying he'd seen many tigers in India but never one as big or as beautiful.

Caldwell suppressed a smile and asked, "So this is a tiger?"

The consul said, "Is it a tiger! Why, man, it is the biggest tiger in creation."

Caldwell said, "Why, that just shows how an ignorant missionary can make a mistake. I have been under the impression that these things were civet cats. Down country we have to chase them out of the back yard every morning. I thought I'd bring one to Foochow just to show you fellows what they look like."

The Chinese laughed heartily, but the consul had no sense of humor and stormed out. Harry's son, John, wrote, "The consul's tiger was large. It was Father's first, and its killing provided him with sweet revenge. From then on no one doubted his tigers, his prowess, or the magic of his gun."

But sometimes the wily tiger turned the tables. One evening, a tiger leaped at Harry as he walked outside his home. He was unarmed but he did have a large, black umbrella, which he aimed at the tiger and opened and shut with a great flapping sound. The tiger fled.

In his last years in Fujian, Caldwell hunted tigers with a camera instead of a gun to capture the great creatures' lives on film. Sadly, they had to flee during the war and most of the footage, obtained at great peril, was lost. But Harry did gain fame for his book, *Blue Tiger*, about the legendary Maltese tiger that he witnessed on a few occasions but was never able to photograph.

A Chinese Boatman's Thanks to America

The Caldwells loved China, and the Chinese also loved the intrepid Tennessee Caldwells. Harry's sons all helped defend their adopted home from the Japanese. Morris, a volunteer fighter pilot, died less than three months after Pearl Harbor while attacking a Japanese cruiser. And the Chinese also loved the intrepid Caldwells from Tennessee.

Harry's son, John, wrote that one of the two people who impressed him most was an uneducated Chinese boatman. John's mother was about to undergo a serious operation in Shanghai and Harry had to find someone to carry him down the roaring Min River to Fuzhou to catch a steamer. But the river was having a record flood and even though he offered a satchel full of silver dollars, no one dared take him. "It's suicide!" they said.

Harry returned home, and as he and the children sat around the table, dejected, they heard a knock at the door. A Chinese soaked by the storm asked, "Are you the American who wishes to go to Fuzhou?"

"Yes, I am," his father said.

"Come," said the man. "I will take you, but we must hurry before the river rises higher." Harry grabbed his satchel full of silver dollars and followed.

For the first seventy-five miles, the boat was tossed like a cork and spun about by vast whirlpools. The helmsman "was lifted off his feet and flung about like a snake is flung by a mongoose." Whenever they completely lost control of the boat, a crewman tossed rice or vegetables overboard, praying fervently to the river gods. At long last, they reached quieter water near Fuzhou, but their troubles weren't over.

The floodwaters were so high that the boat could not pass under the Nantai Island bridge, so the captain hailed a small sampan (a flat-bottomed wooden boat) and urged Harry to quickly board it. Harry did not even have time to ask the captain's name or where he was from, and he'd had no time to negotiate the price, so he handed him the entire satchel full of silver coins. To Harry's surprise, the river boat captain not only refused a single coin but even paid for the sampan fare from his own pocket.

As Harry protested, he said, "Foreign teacher, there is no charge for what I have done today. You were in trouble, you needed to get down the river. I know few things, and have few talents except my knowledge of the river. Those few talents I have are yours to help repay you a little for the things you have done for my people and my country.... I am just a Chinese boatman and this is my thanks to you and to America."

It's no wonder that the Tennessee Caldwells love China and return to visit Kuliang to this day.

CHAPTER EIGHT

General "Vinegar Joe" Stilwell's China

"No more devoted friend of the Chinese people has ever appeared on the pages of history."

—*US Marines General Evans Carlson*

General Joseph Stilwell's grandson, retired Army Colonel John Easterbrook, was unable to join his family at the August 2023 re-opening of Chongqing's newly refurbished Stilwell Museum, so he penned a letter to the Chinese government. To the colonel's surprise, he not only received a letter from President Xi Jinping but, three months later, was invited with his two daughters to meet President Xi at his gathering of "old friends" during the APEC meeting in San Francisco. But the Stilwells were indeed very old friends of China.

President Xi Jinping wrote to Colonel Easterbrook that he was pleased to see even the fifth generation of Stilwell's descendants working towards the cause of China-US friendship. "I truly feel from the Stilwell family the friendly sentiments of the American people toward the Chinese people." Xi praised General Stilwell's contributions to China and declared him an old friend, saying, "The people form the foundation of the China-US relationship . . . and people-to-people friendship is the source of its growth."*

Colonel Easterbrook agreed, commenting on Xi Jinping's letter:

> After all, the more we get to know each other the more we realize that we have much in common with basic wants, needs, and dreams. With that understanding, we can build on common objectives to make the world a better place.†

Home to China

Within only two months of the US establishing relations with China on January 1, 1979, Stilwell's daughter, Alison Stilwell Cameron, who was born in China, visited the land of her birth with her sister Nancy Stilwell Easterbrook. But even through the decades of separation, the sisters had worked to keep alive the Chinese culture and traditions of their childhood. In her youth, Nancy had been the family linguist, perhaps taking after her father, who spoke Japanese, French, Spanish, and Mandarin Chinese, as well as several Chinese dialects. Alison was the family artist. A graduate of Beijing's Peking American School, Alison

---

* Dave Faries and Sara Rubin, "Joseph Stilwell was at home in both Carmel and in China. Now he is a catalyst in a new type of diplomacy," *Monterey County Now*, October 12, 2023

† "To pass down friendship between Chinese, American peoples from generation to generation," *Mero Tribune*, September 5, 2023.

studied Chinese painting under the famous artists Puru (1896-1963), cousin to the last emperor Puyi, and Yu Fei-An (1888-1959), whose painting "Vegetables" was auctioned off at Christies in 2019 for $187, 500. A critic who attended the seventeen-year-old Alison's first one-woman show at the Peking Institute of Fine Arts said she was "the first Occidental to grasp the feeling and technique of Oriental art . . . . "*

The sisters were so moved by the warmhearted reception in China that in 1982 they started the Stilwell Scholarship to help Chinese students pursue a master's degree at Middlebury's Institute of International Studies at Monterey.

Over the years, the sisters raised funds by holding art sales and Chinese New Year dinners, showing China-related films, and leading tour groups to China. Nancy also bequeathed property which was sold after her death in 1987 to fund the scholarship.

The Stilwell Scholarship is now run by Nancy's son, Colonel Easterbrook, who first visited China in 1980. The colonel said, "I would like to call myself an overseer of the scholarship. Keeping it on track is a testimony of the legacy of my grandfather and his respect and admiration of the Chinese people."†

Chinese student Ren Peixi, a recipient of the Stilwell Scholarship, said the scholarship had given her both emotional and financial support, and that she kept in touch with the Stilwells even after graduation, considering them "my relatives in the U.S."‡

---

* "Alison Stilwell Cameron," Northwood University, January 1, 1984 https://www.northwood.edu/archives/945_a/.

† Li Nan, "The Stilwell family's generations of friendship with the Chinese people," *Beijing Review*, January 18, 2024.

‡ Ibid.

In 1991, on the forty-fifth anniversary of Stilwell's death, Nancy Easterbrook and her two children, Nancy and John, attended the opening of China's Stilwell Museum in the general's former home in Chongqing. The 2023 museum reopening, marking the 140th anniversary of Stillwell's birth, was attended by the General's 4th and 5th generation descendants, Susan Mae Easterbrook and Nancy Easterbrook Millward, along with their children, who planted a "friendship tree" with the granddaughter of General Zhu De, whom Stilwell had admired.

But while the Chinese still celebrate Stilwell's contributions, Americans know little about him. As Colonel Easterbrook said, "The Chinese know him better than Americans do."*

General Joseph Stilwell as a young soldier.

* Faries and Rubin, "Joseph Stilwell was at home."

The Stilwell-Chiang Kaishek *Maodun*

Stilwell was a polarizing figure in his day, admired by people such as President Franklin Roosevelt but despised by others—especially "Generalissimo" Chiang Kai-shek. When Chiang demanded yet again that Stilwell be replaced. Roosevelt replied on July 6, 1944:

> The future of all Asia is at stake. . . . I know of no other man who has the ability, the force and the determination to offset the disaster that now threatens China.*

Stilwell was fluent in spoken and written Chinese, knew China more intimately than perhaps any other Western military figure, and was unwavering in what he saw as his duty to both America and China. As Rewi Alley related, Stillwell's stance, in effect, was:

> I am here to fight a war. Because I know something of China and believe in China's potential, the winning of this war is my first duty to the American people. That is what they expect of me. That is why I have been sent here. Those I find opposing my work of winning the war I classify as obstacles to be overcome along with any the enemy puts in my path.†

---

* Charles F. Romanus and Riley Sunderland, *Stilwell's Command Problems* (United States Army, 1956), 383, https://www.ibiblio.org/hyperwar/USA/USA-CBI-Command/USA-CBI-Command-10.html.

† Rewi Alley, *Six Americans in China* (International Culture Publishing Corporation, 1985), 169.

But Chiang Kai Shek was an obstacle not so easily overcome. Stilwell and Chiang epitomized *maodun*, the Chinese phrase for "conflict" meaning "unstoppable spear meets impenetrable shield."

Stilwell had initially believed Chiang was the man to save China from chaos but the generalissimo's refusal to fight the Japanese infuriated him. Chiang, in turn, blamed all of his problems on Stilwell and demanded that Roosevelt replace him. Roosevelt finally caved to Chiang's threats and ultimatums and gave Stilwell, the man he believed to be China's greatest hope, only forty-eight hours to leave the country.

The Chiang-Stilwell *maodun* was rooted in their completely different goals. The US Lend-Lease Act spent $1.6 billion (around $20 billion today) to arm Chiang's Nationalists (Kuomintang/KMT) against Japan, but Chiang repeatedly retreated from the Japanese and hoarded the weapons to use on his political rivals after the war. After Chiang retreated to remote Sichuan on the border of Tibet, as far as he could get from the Japanese, Americans in Guizhou found over twenty KMT warehouses with 50,000 tons of weapons and ammunition stored for use after the war with Japan.

But Stilwell, unlike Chiang, was a born fighter—and from a long line of fighters.

Stilwell's First Steps in Asia

Joe Stilwell was an eighth-generation descendant of English settlers that included a colonel and general who fought in the American Revolution. When asked his ancestry, Joe replied, "Yankee."

Stilwell wanted to study at Yale but his father made him attend West Point in the hopes it would help mature him. In high school, Joe had been the ringleader of boys who engaged in a record number of pranks which led to some students' expulsion; Joe escaped expulsion only because he'd already graduated. And Stilwell did not take West Point any more seriously than high school, setting a record for the number of misbehavior demerits.

General Joseph Stilwell (right) in Burma

Stilwell's only two interests, both of which were to shape his military career, were languages (top of his class in French) and sports such as football and basketball—a new game he introduced to West Point. Joe captained sports teams, set records, and years later adapted his winning football strategies to create brilliant war strategies.

After graduation, Stilwell chose infantry over cavalry because he hated horses. When asked his opinion of using horses in war, he said that horses are "good eating, if you're hungry."*

In June 1904, newly graduated lieutenant Stilwell volunteered to deploy to the last place Americans were still fighting—the

---

* Jennifer McCardle, *"Simulating War: Three Enduring Lessons from the Louisiana Maneuvers," War On the Rocks,* March 17, 2021, https://warontherocks.com/2021/03/simulating-war-three-enduring-lessons-from-the-louisiana-maneuvers/.

Philippines. After "liberating" the Philippines from Spain in 1898, they surprised the Filipinos by refusing to leave. On January 9, 1900, US Senator Albert Beveridge said to the US Senate,

> Mr. President, the times call for candor. The Philippines are ours forever.... And just beyond the Philippines are China's illimitable markets. We will not retreat from either.... The Pacific is our ocean.... China is our natural customer.*

Joe spent fourteen months in the Philippines, where he quickly mastered Spanish well enough to translate documents. He also studied in depth the locals' life and culture—everything from building bamboo bridges (which he taught his troops) to children's games. But given his language skills, in February 1906 he was ordered back to West Point to teach English, French, Spanish, and war tactics.

Joe's sarcasm and harsh criticism of mediocrity quickly earned him the nickname "Vinegar Joe" but Joe loved the moniker, and shared with friends a subordinate's caricature of him rising from a vinegar bottles.† But over time, his concern for soldiers' well-being and no-nonsense informal approach earned the love and respect of both American and Chinese soldiers who took to calling him "Uncle Joe."

---

* Reymann L. Guevarra, "Copy of U.S. Senator Albert J. Beveridge's Speech on Taking the Philippines as a Manifest Duty," at the NHCP Serafin D. Quiason Resource Center, National Historical Commission of the Philippines, February 11, 2025.

† "Gen. Joseph Warren Stilwell Sr.," Honorees, Military Hall of Honor, accessed January 19, 2026, https://militaryhallofhonor.com/honoree-record.php?id=334.

In the summer, Joe traveled to South America in civilian clothes to improve his Spanish and explore Guatemala. He was dismayed at how the corrupt government stole everything the impoverished peasants produced, but he would soon witness far worse conditions in China.

General Joseph Stilwell leads a march in Burma.

Stilwell's First China Visit

In 1910, Joe picked up basic Japanese while touring Japan for a few weeks, and after Winifred sailed home to have their first child, he made his first visit to the US's "natural customer": China.

Although Joe was a military man, in Shanghai he was astonished at the number of foreign warships from Japan, France, England, and the US. He was also surprised that Shanghai's architecture was European, not Asian, and that the police were Indians in turbans. Joe was dismayed at the poverty in the midst of mind-boggling wealth and wrote in his diary that he saw beggars "thick as flies lying in rags in the gutters and groaning.... Vile, filthy canals, clogged with refuse – and yet they live & breed there...selling oranges by the section!"*

* Joe Stilwell, *The Diaries of General Joseph W. Stilwell (1900–1939, 1945–1946)*,

But change was afoot. In 1894, twenty-eight-year-old Western-educated Sun Yat-sen had organized the secret Revive China Society to overthrow the Qing Dynasty. In 1899, US Secretary of State John Hay warned, "The storm center of the world has gradually shifted to China. Whoever understands that mighty empire has the key to the politics of the next 500 years."*

On December 25, 1911, Sun Yat-sen was elected president of the provisional republic and the Empress Dowager abdicated on February 12, 1912. The US congratulated China on its ascension to self-government, but one month later, Sun Yat-sen stepped down and was replaced by Yuan Shikai., who had the military experience that Sun lacked—and the dream of being China's new emperor. He did not last long.

Japan's "One World"

In December 1917, Stilwell was sent to France, but while Westerners wrangled over Europe, Japan leveraged the chaos to fulfill its long-delayed "destiny."

It is claimed that even 2500 years ago, Japan's first emperor, Jinmu-tenno, had a vision of world conquest.† After Toyotomi Hideyoshi (1537–1598) unified Japan, he attacked Korea twice as a steppingstone to China. During the Meiji Restoration (1868–1912), Japan promoted the slogan, "One world, one family" (*Hakko*

Hoover Institution Archives, www.hoover.org.

* Andrew Preston, "America's Pacific Power in a Global Age," The Sea in History—The Modern World, eds. NAM Rodger and Christian Buchet (Boydell & Brewer, 2017), 616-627.

† Zhao Jie Qi, "The formation and expansion of Japanese militarism's ambition for external expansion《日本軍國主義對外擴張野心的形成與膨脹》, *Japan Journal,* April 2005.

ichiu), as justification for a world ruled by a morally and culturally superior Japan. In the twentieth century, Japan capitalized upon Asian's growing anti-western sentiment by promoting "Asia for Asians," which the world soon learned meant "Asia for Japanese."

Japan seized Korea in 1910, and in 1915 demanded that Yuan Shikai give Japan control of China and comply with "Twenty-One Demands" that included forbidding contracts with foreign powers without Japan's consent; acceptance of Japanese military, political, and financial "advisers;" and joint Japanese control of arsenals, police, and schools.* Yuan Shikai accepted most of these demands and, confident that Japan was in his pocket, declared himself China's new emperor. The public was so furious that Yuan stepped down eighty-three days later. Few mourned his death two months later.

As the Allies struggled in Europe, Japan warned it would ally with Germany unless given control of Shandong Province and Germany's pacific islands. Britain, France, and Italy secretly caved to Japan's demands in March 1917, and the US agreed eight months later, the rationale being Japan was so close to Shandong. Not surprisingly, Chinese felt betrayed and refused to sign the Paris Peace Treaty.

After World War I, Stilwell immediately volunteered for an overseas assignment. Given a choice of China or Japan, he chose Japan, but hearing the post was filled, he settled for China and after a year of language training sailed to China in August 1920.

Stilwell was keen on understanding and helping ordinary Chinese, so in 1921 he volunteered to help the Red Cross build an eighty-two-mile road for famine control and relief. As Stilwell

---

* Barbara Tuchman, *Stilwell and the American Experience in China: 1911-1945* (MacMillan, 1971), 61.

worked daily, side-by-side with Chinese laborers, he witnessed desperate poverty that even foreigners living in China knew nothing about, but he admired the people's good humor and persistence even in the face of disaster and chaos. After Stilwell returned to Beijing, he and Winifred resumed life in a foreign legation insulated from the growing mayhem. They enjoyed dinners, sports, and playing Mahjong, but Joe brooded over the knowledge that so many Chinese were dying only a few miles away.

The Break-up of China

"China's Future" was a major topic at the Washington Naval Conference of nine world powers who met from November 1921 to February 1922. Britain's priority had long been maintaining its Asian and African colonies, and had even touted dividing China into European "spheres of influence." In 1899, Lord Charles Beresford had begun his over-four-hundred-page *The Break-up of China* with:

> The break-up of an Empire of four hundred millions of people is an event that has no parallel in history . . . . Investigations on the spot have convinced me that the maintenance of the Chinese Empire is essential to the honor as well as the interests of the Anglo-Saxon race. *

The US, by contrast, had consistently favored China's independence and self-rule. Even two decades later, General Patrick Hurley told Chiang Kai Shek that America wanted a "free, strong, democratic China predominant in Asia."†

---

* Lord Charles Beresford, *The Break-up of China* (Harper & Brothers, 1899), iii-iv.

† Joseph W. Stilwell(ed. Theodore H. White), *The Stilwell Papers*, (Da Capo Press, 1991), 238-240.

Stilwell thought he had put China behind him when he returned to the US in July 1923, but both he and Winifred were delighted to learn of another China assignment and volunteered to return—only to see that China was more chaotic than ever.

On May 30, 1925, British police fired on Chinese students and workers on strike at a Shanghai textile factory, killing thirteen and wounding seventeen. Less than a month later, when Canton workers went on strike to protest the Shanghai massacre, British, French, and Portuguese marines—as well as a British warship—opened fire, killing over fifty unarmed strikers and seriously wounding over 170.

Given the Chinese had no political power in their own country, they hit the British where it hurt most: their purses. Chinese boycotted British goods, and by the end of July, 250,000 Chinese had left Hong Kong, leaving their colonial overlords to fend for themselves. Hong Kong trade fell fifty-percent, shipping fell forty-percent, and Britain spent three million pounds to prevent their colony from collapsing.

But the West's real wake-up call came in July 1925 when the KMT declared itself as the Nationalist Government of China.

The Rise of Chiang Kai-Shek

Western businessmen were furious at Chinese attempts to tax foreign businesses, or to limit such privileges as extrality, which in effect gave all foreigners diplomatic immunity. They blamed missionaries for giving Chinese an education with ideas unsuitable for Asians. As Englishman JOP Bland wrote, "Elected assemblies and democratic institutions are wholly inapplicable, because unintelligible, to the race mind of Asia."*

* J.O.P. Bland, *China: The Pity of It*, (Doubleday, 1932), 256.

Americans, however, supported China's struggle for sovereignty, but had no idea of the gulf between left and right. Chiang Kai Shek soon made it clear that Communists and Nationalists were not simply squabbling political parties like America's Democrats and Republicans.

In 1923, Sun Yat-sen had sent a talented young Chiang Kai-shek to lead a military mission to Moscow. When Sun died in Beijing of cancer in March 1925, Chiang emerged from the power struggle as the KMT leader, but in spite of his Moscow training—or perhaps because of it—he distrusted Communists.

Mao Zedong urged peasants to rise up against ruthless landlords, but Chiang allied himself with the wealthy landlords and businessmen, who in turn funded his crackdown on Communists. From April 12 to 15, 1927, Chiang worked with the Green Gang and French police to kill as many as ten thousand Communists in Shanghai.*

The following month, the Japanese murdered Shandong Province's KMT Commissioner for foreign affairs, along with his wife and fourteen officers. Chiang's response was a "strategic retreat" of his troops to Beijing. But when Japan then seized Manchuria in September 1931, Chiang retreated yet again, even though his forces outnumbered the Japanese. Chiang also ignored Japan's February 1932 proclamation of the independent state of Manchukuo (Manchuria), with Henry Puyi, China's last emperor, as the puppet sovereign. Chiang naively hoped the vast territory of Manchuria would satisfy Japan, seemingly clueless that Japan's goal was all of China, and Asia as well.

When the League of Nations declined to intervene, Chinese

---

* Tom Ryan, Ingrid Purnell, Shivaun Plozza, (eds.), *China Rising: The Revolutionary Experience* (History Teachers' Association of Victoria, 2016), 77.

boycotted Japanese goods. Japan responded by attacking Shanghai's Chinese district on January 29, 1932, slaughtering thousands of Chinese with air raids and troops from warships. Western nations voiced their dismay but did nothing else.

It's important to note that many Japanese civilians knew little of Japan's militancy abroad, and some Japanese leaders and industrialists opposed the actions in China. The Japanese military simply assassinated the dissidents and blamed the US for trying to derail Japan's "destiny" in Asia.

General Stilwell with General Chiang Kai Shek and his wife in 1942.

As Japan expanded its hold on China, Chiang was still fixated on eliminating Communists. In 1934, Chiang sent seven-hundred thousand troops, trained by 400 Nazi advisors he'd hired from Germany, to attack 160,000 Communists. His scorched-earth policy was as brutal as Japan's campaigns, destroying farms and leaving piles of rotting bodies in each village. But as Chiang famously said, he'd "rather mistakenly kill a thousand innocent people than to allow one Communist to escape."*

Some Americans suggested letting Japan have China because the "unlimited markets" Senator Beveridge had touted had not been that profitable. From 1931 to 1935, China's four-hundred million people had accounted for only four percent of US foreign trade—half of what America enjoyed with Japan's much smaller population of seventy million.

Chinese disagreed, however, and when Japan demanded an "autonomous" North China, students protested across China. Japan adroitly changed tactics, portraying itself as anti-communist—which made anyone opposing Japan a communist. Chiang refused to join the so-called "anti-Communist" alliance but he mollified the Japanese by arresting and imprisoning China's anti-Japanese leaders.

On July 7, 1937, Beijing's Marco Polo Bridge incident gave the Japanese the pretext they'd wanted for a "defensive" military campaign. By July 20, Japan had 180,000 troops in the Beijing-Tianjin area, although they reassured a nervous Chiang that Japan merely wanted China's cooperation, not China's land.

As they had done in Korea, Japan destroyed educational centers. On July 29, Japan spent hours bombing Nankai University because it harbored "anti-Japanese elements" (Chinese students). They not only destroyed Hubei University of Medicine but spent an entire week burning books and medical equipment on a massive bonfire.

Meanwhile, back in Beijing, Stilwell reported seeing Chinese students being forced to march in parades celebrating Japan's

* Barbara Barnouin and Yu Changgen, *Zhou Enlai: A Political Life* (Chinese University Press, 2006), 38.

victories, and streamers from balloons that read, "The Japanese Army Preserves the Peace of East Asia."

No Response to Nanjing Massacre

Chiang's refusal to stand up to Japan infuriated Stilwell, but he also predicted the US would continue to complain about Japanese atrocities while doing nothing—which proved true. In December 1937, the Japanese decided to hasten the war's end by making Nanjing an example. At least two-hundred thousand Chinese were murdered during the Nanjing Massacre, with some fifty thousand, 42,000 of them civilians, killed by hand—bayoneting, hacking, burning, raping. Two Japanese lieutenants, Toshiaki Mukai and Tsuyosi Noda, competed to see who could kill a hundred people most quickly with a sword.

On December 12, 1937, Japanese fighters sank the USS Panay gunboat and three Standard Oil Company tankers as they tried to evacuate Americans trapped in Japan's Nanjing invasion. The Japanese even machine-gunned the lifeboats. When the US simply demanded an apology and reparations, the Japanese promptly apologized, saying it was a mistake, even though a Panay officer had informed the Japanese a day earlier of their presence, giant U.S. flags were painted on their awnings, and the aircraft had strafed so low that the victims could see the pilots' faces.*

Unfortunately, the US had reason for its hesitance in confronting Japan. In 1939, the US Army, even with reserves, ranked only seventeenth in size in the world, just behind Portugal.† Even

---

* Richard B. Frank, *Tower of Skulls: A History of the Asia-Pacific War, July 1937-May 1942* (Norton, 2021), 101.

† Rick Atkinson, "Ten things every American student should know about our army in World War II," Foreign Policy Research Institute, May 28, 2009.

worse, Germany had accomplished more in six weeks than it had in four years of World War I, yet, as Stilwell complained, the US was not learning from their example.

The Shift from "Europe First"

Stilwell had been promoted to brigadier general in July 1939, and in 1940 was promoted to major general right after Japan joined the Axis—which Stilwell had predicted much earlier. But to Stilwell's frustration, the US focus remained "Europe first" because Westerners believed that Europe would always be the center of world power. In 1941 the West learned to take Asia more seriously.

On the sleepy Sunday morning of December 7, 1941, Japan shocked the world with its devastating attack on Pearl Harbor. On the same day, Japan also bombed Hong Kong, Guam, Wake Island, and Malaya. On December 10, Japan sunk Britain's two newest battleships in Malaya. On December 11, at Japan's request, Germany and Italy declared war on the US.

On January 2, 1942, the Philippines, which Senator Beveridge had proclaimed was "ours forever," surrendered to Japan.

Japan overpowered Asia so rapidly because its navy was as large as the combined navies of the US, Britain, and the Netherlands—ten battleships, ten carriers, and five hundred planes. The US, by contrast, had one undamaged and two slightly damaged battleships and three carriers.

Stilwell, meanwhile, had been sent to Africa to spearhead the US's first offensive of World War II, but he and Roosevelt both worried about China.

Although Roosevelt's grandfather, Warren Delano, Jr. (1809–1898), had made the family fortune smuggling opium into China, Roosevelt vehemently opposed colonialism and believed that the right of people to choose their own form of government "was as applicable to the peoples of Asia as to those of Europe."* Roosevelt admired the Chinese's courage, and on April 28, 1942, declared:

> We remember that the Chinese people were the first to stand up and fight against the aggressors in this war; and in the future, an unconquerable China will play its proper role in maintaining peace and prosperity not only in Eastern Asia but in the whole world.†

But Roosevelt's preoccupation with China irked Churchill. Roosevelt had led the US to end Americans' extraterritorial rights in China, and Churchill reluctantly agreed to help repeal the West's unequal treaties with China—though he drew a line with Hong Kong. Churchill wrote to one of his generals:

> I must enlighten you upon the American view. China bulks as large in the minds of many of them as Great Britain.... If I can epitomize in one word the lesson I learned in the United States, it was 'China.'‡

---

* Foster Rhea Dulles and Gerald E. Ridinger, "The Anti-Colonial Policies of Franklin D. Roosevelt," *Political Science Quarterly* 70, no. 1 (March 1955): 1-18, https://doi.org/10.2307/2145412.

† *Department of State Bulletin, May 2, 1942, p. 381;* also, https://www.presidency.ucsb.edu/documents/fireside-chat-5

‡ James Bradley, *The China Mirage: The Hidden History of American Disaster in Asia* (Little, Brown, 2015), 300.

On January 1, 1942, General George Marshall sent for Stilwell to hear why he thought the war's focus should shift from Europe to Asia. When Stilwell was asked to return to China, he agreed, but knowing that Chiang would never fight the Japanese, he asked to be given command of Chinese troops. Chiang, however, would only accept as commander an American who was a lieutenant general or higher. So, in February 1942 they promoted Stilwell to lieutenant general and made him head of US forces in India and China. A *New York Times* article proclaimed, "General Looks to 'Happiest Day' When Chinese and U.S. Troops Will Enter Tokyo."*

General Joseph Stilwell late in his distinguished career.

* *New York Times*, March 21, 1942.

Tokyo seemed as far off as ever when Chiang not only refused to fight the Japanese but refused to give Stilwell troops, and, when he did finally received the promised troops, the Nationalist officers refused to obey him.

A "Simple Plan" to Defeat Japan

Chiang and Roosevelt were both relieved when, on October 8, 1942, General Claire Chennault of Flying Tigers fame promised that if he were made commander of the US military in China, he could defeat Japan six months to a year with only 105 modern fighters and thirty medium and twelve heavy bombers:

> Japan can be defeated in China. It can be defeated by an Air Force so small that in other theaters it would be called ridiculous .... I am now confident that given full authority as the American military commander in China that I can not only bring about the downfall of Japan but that... I can create such good will that China will be a great and friendly trade market for generations.*

Although Roosevelt was elated, Stilwell thought Chennault's ridiculously easy plan was ridiculously naïve, saying Chennault had only seen China from the air, whereas he himself had traveled overland through most of the country, and understood the massive ground support needed for such an operation.

As Stilwell had predicted, it took much more than 147 aircraft and a year to defeat Japan. Japan's defeat took three more years, with nine armies from India, China, the Pacific, and Alaska, a naval air force in 1945 of ninety carriers and 14,847 combat aircraft.

---

* Bradley, *The China Mirage*, 300.

Although Roosevelt had agreed to the Flying Tigers scheme, he rejected giving up Stilwell's command. He told Chiang to stop hiding and use his forces, and America's billions in aid, to finally attack the Japanese. He also told Chiang to put all troops under Stilwell's command—otherwise, China was lost. Chiang was furious—especially when he learned Stilwell wanted to arm his enemies.

Arming Chiang's Enemy

Stilwell had given up on the Nationalists ever fighting but he was impressed with the Communists' Eighth Route Army leadership and Zhou Enlai. Some of their strategies were so effective that General Carlson later adapted them for the US Marines. It was no wonder that Stilwell said if China ever defeated Japan, there would be issues between the Communists and the KMT, and it was clear who would win.

General Zhu De and Mao Zedong sent greetings to Stilwell and assured him that they would fight under his command but not under any Chinese general appointed by Chiang. In December, 1944, Stilwell cabled army chief of staff Marshall, saying, "Somehow we must get arms to the Communists who will fight."* After Stilwell's death, he was accused of Communist sympathies, but his motives were pragmatic, not political. The Communists were the only Chinese he could rely upon to fight. Even Claire Chennault at one point told Roosevelt the Communists and Nationalists needed to fight together.

In Chiang's mind, however, arming his political rivals was the last straw. After Chiang had fired off a barrage of threats and

---

* Michael Schaller, *The US Crusade in China, 1938–1945* (Columbia University Press, 1982), 168-169.

ultimatums, Roosevelt gave Stilwell forty-eight hours to get out of China. Undeterred, Stilwell sent John Service to Washington to reaffirm why the US should fight side-by-side with the Communists—a move that cost John Service his reputation and career.

In Stilwell's rushed last hours in China, he penned a letter to Claire Chennault. In spite of their differences, Stilwell admired him as a fellow fighter and praised Chennault's achievements, and assured him that the Chinese also admired him. Stilwell also wrote to the Communist General Zhu De to express his "keen disappointment" that he would not be able to fight with him and his fine soldiers against the Japanese.

A bust of General Stilwell stands at the Stillwell Museum in Chongqing.

After returning home, Stilwell wrote a seven-hundred-page report about his experiences but it was not published because he refused to tone down his criticism of Chiang and the British. Even so, Stilwell was confident the American public would eventually realize Chiang was not a champion of democracy but a dictator. He was wrong, but did not live to see it.

"Vinegar Joe" died on October 12, 1946, after surgery for stomach cancer—just five months before retirement. As he had predicted, the Communists and KMT waged a civil war and Chiang lost. But he might have been chagrined to learn that after fleeing to Taiwan and establishing history's second longest military dictatorship, Chiang was still hailed as a champion of democracy.

But were "Vinegar Joe" here today, he would at least be proud that five generations of his descendants have worked to build friendships and understanding between the US and China. In September 2023, a few weeks after the reopening of Chongqing's Stilwell Museum, "Vinegar Joe's" great-granddaughter, Nancy Easterbrook Millward, joined Nicholas Burns, US Ambassador to China, on a National Public Radio interview. Nancy said of her great grandfather's legacy:

> I hope this sort of inspires people to look at history, the good things that happened during a very awful time, during World War II, and just remember that that's possible. We can get back to being good allies and good friends and learn from each other's cultures.*

* John Ruwitch, "Despite strained relations, US and China still pay tribute to Gen. Joseph Stilwell," NPR Morning Edition, September 14, 2023.

CHAPTER NINE

John Service
China-Born American Patriot

"The Communists are in China to stay and China's destiny is not Chiang's but theirs."

—John Service's official report comparing Communist-held Yan'an with the rest of China

Had the US read the report that General Stilwell had John Service take to Washington, China's history might have been very different. But the report was ignored, and not forwarded to Washington for two months, by which time China had lost its last hope of avoiding a civil war. But Service could have never imagined that his report would destroy his career and life.

When Service met Mao and Zhou, the enemy was the Nazis,

not the Communists. The Communist Soviets, after all, were allies, and made the greatest sacrifices to defeat Hitler. Some twenty-seven million Soviets died, and a quarter of the population was killed or wounded.

After disregarding Service's report, the US sent General Patrick J. Hurley to help unite the Communists and Nationalists, even though Hurley was so ignorant of China that he thought the Communists and Nationalists were simply two political parties such as America's Republicans and Democrats. Not surprisingly, Hurley failed—and blamed Service for his failure.

John Service, one of the few Americans who understood and loved both China and the US, became the first of Senator Joseph McCarthy's thousands of victims in the Red Scare of the 1950s. Service was branded a traitor, arrested, and jailed. Even though he was eventually acquitted, he was fired for his "disloyalty," and spent the rest of his life trying to recover his reputation.

China-Born US Diplomat

John was born in 1909 in West China's ancient city of Chengdu, a city so remote that his six-month-old sister, Virginia, died during the family's arduous three-month trip from the coast. His parents were missionaries who started Sichuan's YMCA, which was later popular with progressive students demanding reform. The family lived in a typical Chinese home within a walled courtyard, and John grew up speaking the local Sichuan dialect with his young Chinese friends. But even to young John, it was obvious that the ancient empire of China was dying.

China had been crumbling since the nineteenth century when Britain's opium wars forced the opium trade on Chinese. And the Qing Dynasty's collapse in 1911, when John was two-years-old, forced the country into even greater chaos.

In spite of the turmoil, the Service family stuck to their mission in Chengdu. By age ten, young John was fluent in the local language, had finished eight grades of school by correspondence, and could walk thirty miles a day. At age eleven he was sent to the Shanghai American School, although he returned home for the summer and celebrated his twelfth birthday hiking for six days to a fifteen-thousand-foot Tibetan pass.

In 1927, John entered Ohio's Oberlin College and majored in art history and economics. He was also captain of two record-setting sports teams. He explained the spirit that drove him in both sports and life. "It's not merely a matter of who's the best runner or the stronger, but who's got the most determination, resolve, and guts."*

While John studied at Oberlin, the land of his birth continued to deteriorate. Chiang Kai-shek allied with the Communists to attack warlords and imperialists, and told them to seize Wuhan. But on the night of April 12, 1927, Chiang's forces secretly entered Shanghai with ruthless gunmen of the Green Gang (a network of secret societies, gangsters, and opium smugglers), and murdered as many as ten-thousand of their unsuspecting Communist "allies."† The KMT also murdered over a hundred students and workmen who protested against the violence

Another million Chinese were murdered around the country during Chiang's campaign to kill Communists and Communist sympathizers. Chiang's troops also executed many women with unbound feet and short hair, as this, too, set a radical and dangerous precedent.

---

* Lynne Joiner, *Honorable Survivor: Mao's China, McCarthy's America, and the Persecution of John S. Service* (Naval Institute Press, 2009), 13.

† Ryan, *China Rising*, 77.

Meanwhile, back in the US, John Service and his sweetheart Caroline graduated from college in 1931, but given the Great Depression's lack of jobs, John studied art history for a year with the hopes of eventually becoming a professor. While John pursued his studies, the Japanese seized Manchuria, and on January 18, 1932, Japanese marines murdered eighteen-thousand Chinese civilians in Shanghai. Chinese were furious but Westerners shrugged it off—except for John, who vowed to return to China as soon as possible.

John was anxious to get back to China and crammed for two months to pass the two-day written exam for the US Foreign Service. He easily passed the oral exams in January 1933 but was not given a job because of a hiring freeze. Undaunted, John returned to Shanghai with his father and landed a job as a clerk in the smallest and remotest US consulate in Yunnan, just south of his birth province of Sichuan.

In November 1933, John met up with Caroline in Vietnam and after being married by a French mayor, they took the three-day train to Yunnan. John had promised Caroline and her parents that she would love Yunnan, even though it was not quite like Shanghai, the "Paris of the East." But Catherine hated Yunnan. They had to share a house with no electricity or running water, and few Americans to socialize with. She finally moved to stay with John's parents in Shanghai, returning six months later after John was promoted to vice-consul and had his own home. Although life in Yunnan was difficult, John credited the experience with giving him the training and skills that made him effective later as a Foreign Service Officer.

In the spring of 1935, foreigners began circulating rumors of an invasion by Communists fleeing Chiang Kai-shek, but John also understood the Chinese peasants' rumors and was intrigued to hear that the Communists soldiers were disciplined and treated farmers respectfully, even paying for provisions, whereas Nationalist soldiers simply seized anything they wanted, be it food, clothing, or the farmer's daughter.

In 1935, John was finally hired by the US Foreign Service and, to his wife's relief, was sent to Beijing for intensive language study. Catherine enjoyed Beijing's expat life and hobnobbing it with diplomats, and John put his "grit" into mastering Beijing Chinese, though he was criticized for his rural Sichuan accent.

In the fall of 1936, the Services invited friends to their home to hear a talk by an American journalist, Edgar Snow, who had defied Chiang Kai-shek's ban and visited the Communists in their Yan'an stronghold. Snow was impressed by the great contrast between the lives of Chinese in Yan'an and the rest of China, and further infuriated Chiang Kai-shek by publishing *Red Star Over China*.

But even Chiang's own Nationalist troops were tiring of his fixation with eliminating Communists while ignoring Japan, the real enemy. When Chiang ordered his men to carry out another massacre of suspected Communists, they kidnapped Chiang instead. On the evening of December 12, 1936, four trucks carrying 120 soldiers stopped outside Chiang's hotel and gunned down his bodyguards. Chiang escaped over a wall but was found four hours later with a sprained ankle and shivering in a cold cave. The soldiers took turns carrying him down the hill.

Chiang's kidnappers demanded an end to the civil war; a new united, democratic government that included Communist and Nationalist representatives; and a united army under Chiang's command to fight the Japanese instead of each other. Hopeful Chinese students across the country joined the soldiers in demanding "Unity!" Zhou Enlai had almost perished in Chiang's Shanghai massacre (April 12, 1927), but he kept his feelings to himself and urged Chiang to join a united front against the Japanese.

Seven months later, from his Beijing apartment, John Service heard the gunbattle on the Marco Polo Bridge that started an eight-year war with Japan. The Japanese murdered tens of thousands as they expanded control of North China and murdered over three-hundred thousand Chinese in the Nanjing Massacre.

In 1940, Service helped evacuate his family and others, and then immediately volunteered for dangerous duty in his birthplace of Sichuan, arriving just as the embassy people were evacuated. John met both Zhou Enlai and Chiang Kai-shek. Chiang maintained the facade of a united front with the Communists against the Japanese but was increasingly jealous of the Communists' growing reputation—especially after the widespread praise of their daring simultaneous attack behind Japanese enemy lines in five provinces.

Even in remote Sichuan, Service heard complaints about Chiang. He also saw that many who questioned Chiang, including well-known professors, vanished, never to be seen again.

Any hope of true unity against the Japanese was destroyed in January 1941 when Chiang ordered the Communists to retreat north of the Yangtze River. They obeyed, but one group—which included women, children, and the wounded—lagged behind. Chiang murdered thousands of them and took thousands prisoner.

In July, the Japanese murdered twenty million Chinese in occupied North China. Western media remained largely silent—until the attack on Pearl Harbor. Mao Zedong immediately urged all Chinese to support the Americans and British in fighting Japan, but Chiang's priority remained unchanged—the destruction of his political rivals, rather than the Japanese.

General Stilwell, one of the few American generals brave enough to fight the war with Japan from the frontlines, met with Chiang and said he was "courteous, friendly, and plan-less," and that "Chiang's top priority was not saving China from Japan but "maintaining control over his best troops and their supplies to prevent rivals from threatening his position as supreme leader."*

John Service and his wife in China in 1934.

---

* Joiner, *Honorable Survivor*, 29.

One of President Roosevelt's assistants warned him that Chiang was no longer even pretending to have a democratic government. And Chiang's wife, Mei-ling, darling of American media, was as ruthless as her husband. At a dinner in DC, Mei-ling was asked how her government would handle such trouble as US labor leaders. She silently drew her finger across her own throat, prompting Eleanor Roosevelt to later say, "She can talk beautifully about democracy, but she does not know how to *live* democracy."*

But this did not stop President Roosevelt from standing at a press conference with Mei-ling at his side and declaring, "China [under Chiang] has become one of the great democracies of the world."

While Western politicians and media praised Chiang and Mei-ling, Americans like General Stilwell and John Service urged Washington to cease its blind support of Chiang and to visit the Communists in Yan'an to see the truth of Chiang's so-called united front.

Zhou Enlai promised the US military his cooperation against the Japanese, so Stilwell made John Service his political advisor, as well as his special liaison to the Chinese Communists. Communist reports on Japanese forces quickly proved far more reliable than Nationalist reports. John also learned of atrocities that Chiang's censor machine had silenced. For example, as many as five-hundred to seven-hundred thousand Chinese, already struggling with the Nationalists' taxes, died from famine, disease, and flooding after Chiang flooded the Yellow River to stop advancing Japanese.

In an official report, Service warned, "China is dying a lingering death by slow strangulation," and explained why Chiang was

---

* Joiner, *Honorable Survivor*, 40.

as much to blame as the Japanese for China's military, economic, and political disaster. Only true democratic political reform, Service warned, could unify China and create a government that the people would support. Otherwise, China would have a civil war that Chiang could not win.

Many Chinese and foreigners in China shared Service's opinion, but only Service was brave enough—or foolish enough—to not only criticize Chiang but also condemn the haphazard and inept operations of various US intelligence operations in China. He urged the US to stop collaborating with Nationalist secret police who interrogated and tortured political prisoners, and to cease its blind, unconditional support of the Nationalists. Yet at the same time, Service also made clear that his goal was not to overthrow Chiang, but to force him to adopt a more just and democratic government. If Chiang had any vision at all, Service said, he would see this would guarantee him even greater popular support and the power needed to unite China.

Sadly, Service's honest and heartfelt report would later be used to arrest him on charges of treason.

When Service finally joined the Dixie Mission to spend three months in Yan'an and discover the truth about the unknown Communists, the entire team was astonished at the contrast between Yan'an and the rest of China. Service wrote, "We are coming into a different country and meeting a different people."

Unlike the rest of China, the Communists had no desperate poverty or beggars. People lived very simply, but their "cave" homes had gardens. The people elected their own leaders, and Service wrote, "Morale is very high. There is no defeatism, but rather confidence." And whereas Nationalist soldiers lived off the peasants, the Communists soldiers helped farmers develop land and even grew their own food.

John Service greeting Zhou Enlai.

On August 22, a month after the Dixie Mission's arrival in Yan'an, Service met Mao for eight hours in his cave-dwelling and Mao explained that the Communists not only wanted to help the US fight against Japan but also hoped for US aid in helping to unify China under a broader, more democratic government.

By night, Service pecked away at his typewriter, sharing his careful observations—totally ignorant that his reports would be largely ignored. And shortly after the War, Service's report would be used as ammunition to show that he was a "Communist sympathizer." But as he said later in his trial, at that time the Communists were being courted as allies. Japanese and Nazis, not Communists, were the enemy—so Service, perhaps naively, had no qualms reporting with admiration the startling difference between Mao's and Chiang's two Chinas.

The "Loss" of China

Service was fired in 1951 because of "reasonable doubts as to his loyalty." Many of McCarthy's allegations were later proven to be false, but it was too late to help Service—whom the FBI hounded for over two decades—or the hundreds who were imprisoned and the ten thousand to twelve thousand who lost their jobs.

Service was hired again by the State Department in 1957, but in spite of being judged innocent of all charges, and receiving excellent performance reviews in every position, he was never again promoted.

Even when he was put in charge of the US consulate in Liverpool, he did not receive a title or pay raise.

John finally retired in 1962, earned a Master of Arts degree in political science from the University of California, Berkeley, and worked as library curator for the school's Center for Chinese Studies.

In 1971, the year before President Nixon's visit to China, China invited Service and a few other Americans to visit. Service met with Zhou Enlai, and he and his wife appeared on the cover of *Parade*.

On January 30, 1973, the US State Department held a very special luncheon in honor of John Service and other Foreign Service officers who had been vilified in the 1950s for having "lost" China to the Communists. Yet even then, many American politicians were outraged at honoring Service, who had been high on McCarthy's list of American communists in the State Department. Some brought up the old but disproven allegation that Service had been caught red-handed slipping secret material to an identified Communist. And even just before the banquet honoring the long-suffering Service, someone put anonymous leaflets on every table accusing Service of traitorous activities.

John Service, then sixty-three, kept his cool, and with the same calm demeanor that had won both admiration and hatred on both sides of the Pacific, he said:

> There are still countries—in Latin America, Africa, and parts of Asia—where the situation is not unlike that in China during the 1940s. If we keep ourselves in ignorance and out of touch with new popular movements and potentially revolutionary situations, we may find ourselves again missing the boat.... The legacy of Senator Joe McCarthy still needs, in some respects, to be shed.*

The persecution of John Service is told in *Honorable Survivor.*

John Service's dispatches are collected in *Lost Chance in China*, an inside account of wartime policy.

---

* Joiner, *Honorable Survivor*, xvi-xvii.

In 2009, after twenty years of research and even visiting China with Service, Lynne Joiner published her long-awaited biography, *Honorable Survivor: Mao's China, McCarthy's America, and the Prosecution of John S. Service*. Published by the Naval Institute Press, this insightful work not only explores the causes of the Cold War but also shows those same forces are profiting to this day by keeping China and the US at odds with each other, even though, as Service said almost a century ago, both nations would benefit far more if we worked together instead of against each other.

CHAPTER TEN

George Hatem (Ma Haide)

Chinese People's American Doctor

When Chinese media announced the passing of Dr. Ma Haide on October 3, 1988, few people outside of China knew that Dr. Ma had been born Shafick George Hatem, of Lebanese-American parents in the US.

Hatem was a legend even in international medical circles for devoting over half a century of his life to improving China's medical care. In 1986, Hatem received the Albert Lasker Public Service Award,

> For legendary contributions to the control and eradication of venereal diseases and leprosy in China, greatly improving the health of a billion people.... Dr. Ma's contributions can be compared in importance to the eradication of yellow fever and the bubonic plague, and, as a

model for the public health control of venereal diseases, they stand alone.*

Hatem also helped launch China's "barefoot doctors," a program so efficient and cost-effective that the US Department of Health, Education, and Welfare in 1974 published a 950-page English version of China's *Barefoot Doctor's Manual*, noting in its preface how China's army of some two million medical workers had served the world's largest population with both Western medicine and "treatments and remedies developed in China over the span of a thousand years."

But how did this young Lebanese American become a doctor and end up in China?

Becoming Ma Haide

In 1902, George's Maronite father, Nahoum, moved from Lebanon to Massachusetts to work in a textile mill. In 1909, Nahoum returned to Lebanon to marry and then got a job in a steel mill in Buffalo, New York. George was born on September 26, 1910 in Buffalo—where he also met the man who inspired him to become a doctor.

When every person in George's impoverished family of six caught the Spanish flu, an elderly doctor not only met their medical needs but also supplied them with food for several months until Nahoum was well enough to work again. George said, "I thought this doctor was the most wonderful man in the world, and I wanted to be like him. Workers' are always scared of sickness, for if the breadwinner cannot work, the whole family goes hungry."

---

* Renamed the Lasker-Bloomberg Public Service Award in 2009.

Hatem's family moved to South Carolina to open a dry goods store and George graduated valedictorian in the 1927 class of Greenville High School (today, Greenville Senior High School). He then pursued his calling of medicine with pre-med classes at the University of North Carolina, and a scholarship made possible his medical studies at the American University of Beirut from 1929 to 1931 and the University of Geneva, where he received his medical degree in 1933 at the age of twenty-two. George had befriended Chinese students in Geneva, and when he heard of China's health challenges, he and two other young American doctors sailed to Shanghai in 1933 for one year of medical practice and research on ending tropical diseases such as leprosy and eradicating venereal diseases.

That "one year" would become a China medical practice of over half a century.

Hatem's initial focus had been medical research and the eradication of leprosy and other tropical diseases, as well as venereal diseases (especially widespread in Shanghai, which had a brothel on virtually every corner). But Hatem was appalled by workers' conditions he witnessed on factory inspection tours in Shanghai, so he expanded his medical care to Chinese workers, volunteering in two large hospitals to help poor patients.

Rewi Alley wrote that Hatem "was never a fanatic, never a starry-eyed idealist." He lived a quiet, unassuming, happy life, but as he came to better understand China's situation, he quickly grew disillusioned and indignant at how Western nations ignored the gangsterish corruption and the unimaginable suffering of Chinese even in the wealthiest cities. Alley wrote:

> In Shanghai, he had a close inside look at imperial occupation; the spectacle of Battleship Row anchored on the

> Huangpu opposite the big banks of the Bund, well-fed Western businessmen and their sleek wives dancing in evening clothes at the French Club, and then the starving Chinese rickshaw pullers openly beaten on the streets by the foreign concession police.

George was slowly realizing that medical care was just a bandage on an open wound, and that China needed fundamental change, when he met three people who would heavily influence his future: New Zealand activist Rewi Alley, journalist Agnes Smedley, and Sun Yat-sen's widow, Soong Ching-ling.

By 1936, Hatem was frustrated at the little impact his medical practice was making. Treating venereal disease was very profitable for Shanghai doctors, but he'd moved to China intent on bringing change, not just "mopping up" after prostitutes and their Johns. Edgar Snow quoted Hatem as once saying, "I didn't spend my old man's money learning to become a VD [venereal disease] quack for a gangster society."*

Dr. Ma Haide, 1937

Hatem decided to abandon his medical practice and find a better way to bring about change. He considered moving to Spain to help the Republicans in the Civil War against General Francisco Franco (who would triumph and become Spain's dictator until his death in 1975). But Soong Ching-ling had other ideas. Soong opposed the Nationalists, even though

* Walter Sullivan, "Dr. George Hatem Is Dead at 78; Leader in Public Health in China." *New York Times*, October 6, 1988.

she was the sister of Mei-ling, Chiang Kai-shek's wife, and Soong Ai-ling, wife of China's richest man, H. H. Kung, who influenced Nationalist economic policies. Soong Ching-ling helped Hatem see that China had even greater needs than Spain—and greater hope.

As Hatem grew to understand the depths of China's darkness and corruption, he wrote articles for various publications, including the *Voice of China* (中国呼声), which was published in English in Shanghai, supported by Soong Ching-ling, and edited by Snow, Smedley, Alley, and others. Not surprisingly, the *Voice of China* infuriated both the Japanese and Chiang Kai-shek's Nationalists.

In the spring of 1936, the Chinese Communists had asked for an impartial foreign journalist and medical doctor to visit their headquarters in northern Shaanxi to inspect their situation and better understand why they were calling for China to unite in its resistance against the Japanese. Soong Ching-ling recommended George Hatem and Edgar Snow. Hatem had no idea he was leaving his Shanghai medical practice for good when friends smuggled him and Snow across the Nationalist lines to Yan'an. Hatem could barely speak a word of Chinese and had to rely on Snow to communicate for him.

Hatem and Snow traveled by truck and then on foot with a guide and a donkey to carry their gear, including Hatem's medical supplies. They were fascinated by the unearthly, treeless loess landscape, and the peasants "cave" homes. In some areas, entire villages had been dug into the hillsides.

After walking for two days, Snow and Hatem finally reached a village where they were greeted in English by Zhou Enlai. Hatem and Snow were impressed by the erudite Zhou.

After another two-day journey on horseback, Snow and Hatem reached Bao'an, where the two were given a room in the *waijiaobu* ("foreign office")—very simple accommodations, but far better than they'd enjoyed during the trip.

Although many of the soldiers were ill, their clothing was in tatters, and their numbers so few, Hatem and Snow were surprised by the troops' and villagers' good humor and optimism, which they had not seen anywhere else in China. It reminded George of the spirit of early American pioneers who banded together to overcome seemingly impossible obstacles. George recalled decades later, "You could have assembled the whole Red Army on an area no larger than a football field, but they were so confident and optimistic they caused me to believe in them altogether."*

They asked to visit the Red Army on the frontlines and on August 16 arrived at the Red Army headquarters in Ningxia—where George Hatem became Ma Haide.

The Ningxia locals, most of whom were Muslim Hui minority, were surprised that Hatem could read and write some Arabic. Although his family was Maronite Christian from Lebanon, George knew some Islamic practices. Dai Jimin, the Red Army doctor, was also Hui, and Hatem and Jimin quickly gained the people's trust. When Hatem learned that nine of ten Hui were surnamed *Ma* ("horse"), he strengthened his bond with them by changing his own name to Ma Haide. Many locals assumed Ma Haide was Turkish, and Shanghai newspapers began reporting that the Communists had a Turkish doctor—clueless that it was the former Shanghai doctor Hatem.

Edgar Snow finished his interviews and prepared to leave, determined to share their story with the world. But to his surprise, the quiet, modest Hatem announced he would stay on and use his medical skills to help the fledgling movement.

---

* Rewi Alley, *Six Americans in China* (China Books & Periodicals, 1985), 10.

Mao Zedong appreciated Hatem's pragmatic suggestions to improve health care and made him public health adviser to the CPC's Central Military Commission. In February 1937, Hatem became the first foreigner to join the CPC to underscore that he was no longer an outsider but committed to the end, regardless of the outcome. After working at Eighth Route Army headquarters, Hatem returned to Yan'an to prepare for the construction of the Shaanxi-Gansu-Ningxia Border Region Hospital. And to better understand the people he had committed his life to, he not only rapidly learned Mandarin Chinese but surprised locals by even mastering the North Shaanxi dialect.

Dr. Haide with Mao Zedong, 1944.

As casualties mounted, Hatem appealed to Soong Ching-ling and others back in Shanghai to send more doctors, one of whom would be the Canadian surgeon Norman Bethune. In Canada, Bethune had objected to medical care being treated as a luxury. He promoted socialized medicine and went in search of the poor to provide them free medical care. He then served as a frontline surgeon on the Republican side during the Spanish Civil War.

In July 1937, shortly before leaving for Spain, Bethune wrote for the *Canadian Forum* a poem that ended with: "Comrades, who fought for freedom and the future world, Who died for us, we will remember you."*

Bethune himself would join those fallen comrades less than two years later.

In January 1938, Bethune moved to China and helped Hatem bring medical care to Chinese troops and peasants. Bethune trained doctors, nurses, and orderlies, and in performing battlefield surgeries, he treated patients from either side of the conflict.

On November 12, 1939, Bethune died following an infection contracted while treating wounded soldiers. The day before he died, he wrote in his last will, "Dear Commander Nie, Today I feel really unwell. Probably I have to say farewell to you forever!"

Mao Zedong wrote a eulogy for Bethune, who is honored to this day not only in China but in Canada. His Ontario birthplace is now the Bethune Memorial House, and in March 1990 on the centenary of Bethune's birth, both China and Canada issued identical postage stamps in his honor.

George Hatem was dismayed by Bethune's death, yet pressed on. But his life was brightened considerably in 1940 when he met and married the beautiful Chinese actress, Zhou Sufei ("Sophie" 周苏菲). George's Chinese was still not that good when he met Sufei. He told Alley, "I suddenly discovered I had a lot to say to her and no words to say it. My vocabulary was still mostly limited to such phrases as 'Where does it hurt?' Any fever?' George took an intensive six-months language course and by the end could speak fairly fluent Chinese on many subjects—including marriage. Mao Zedong and Zhou

---

* Norman Bethune, "Red Moon," *Canadian Forum* [Toronto] July 1937.

Enlai attended the wedding. Once married, George learned some acting, even playing a part in an opera, and Sufei learned enough medicine that her fellow performers came to her for medical advice.

As if Hatem's medical duties were not enough, Hatem continued to promote China's cause to the rest of the world—although the Nationalists and the Japanese both tried to silence the *Voice of China*.

The Kuomintang had been confiscating as many copies of the *Voice of China* as they could find and arresting anyone found distributing it. Chiang also forced the U.S. Consulate to cancel its registered trade name. The *Voice of China* also infuriated the Japanese. In August 1937, the Japanese invaded Shanghai and one of their first moves was to locate and destroy the *Voice of China*'s typesetting workshop. The *Voice of China* was silenced, but in November, Hatem helped Xinhua News Agency establish its English Department and began to broadcast English news abroad about the atrocities being committed by the Japanese across the country—but even Hatem could not have guessed at the horrors ahead.

On August 5, 1937, the Japanese emperor had decreed that Japan was no longer bound by international law in the treatment of Chinese prisoners. In December, the Japanese prince, General Yasuhiko Asaka, led his troops on the 170-mile march from Shanghai to Nanjing, where he ordered his troops to "kill all captives." Some three-hundred thousand Chinese, mostly civilians, died in the Nanjing Massacre, and up to ten million more Chinese, mostly civilians, perished before the war was over. But after the war, neither prince nor Emperor were tried for war crimes because General MacArthur had granted immunity to the entire Japanese royal family.

Hatem continued to work with scalpel in one hand, pen in the other. In addition to frequent reports to Soong Ching-ling, he also appealed for international assistance. In 1944, when General Joseph Stilwell sent a US military observation team to inspect the true situation in Yan'an, Hatem served as the consultant of the US military observation team. Hatem knew the situation like no one else. Between 1944 and 1947 alone, he treated over forty thousand sick and wounded patients.

After a bloody civil war, Chiang Kai-shek and the Nationalists retreated to Taiwan and in October 1949, Hatem was invited to Tiananmen for the founding ceremony of the People's Republic of China. In 1950, Hatem became a Chinese citizen, and was appointed Medical Consultant of the Ministry of Health. He helped establish the Central Dermato-Venereology Institute and led a campaign to eliminate not only venereal disease but also the rampant prostitution that had so dismayed him in Shanghai.

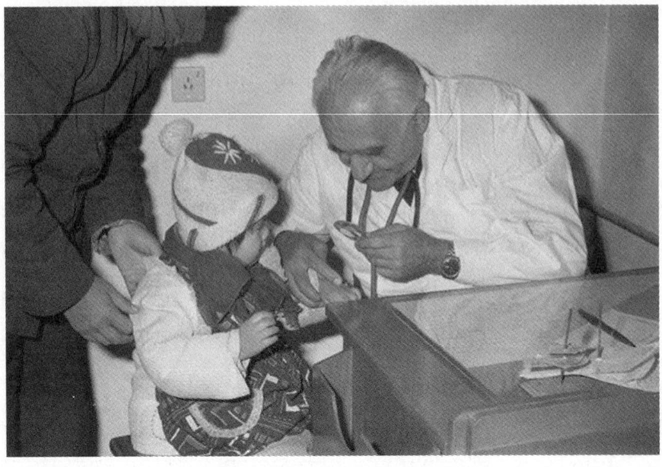

Dr. Haide with a young patient.

Hatem worked with experts across China, visiting Inner Mongolia, Yunnan, Guizhou, Sichuan, Guangdong, Guangxi,

Jiangsu, Jiangxi, Tibet, and Xinjiang. Like China's army of barefoot doctors, Hatem lived with the people he treated, whether in a yurt, an old temple or a run-down hotel in which he shared a moth-eaten blanket with several people. When conducting tests in remote areas that lacked electricity for his dark-field microscope, he modified the microscope to use dry cell batteries.

Dr. Haide with his wife, Chou Sufei, in 1944.

The peasants at first refused to allow doctors to withdraw blood for tests, so Hatem had doctors take samples of his own blood to prove its safety. He laughed and joked with the peasants, and even sang with them. His calm, gentle demeanor and compassion gained the people's trust, and helped China to make great achievements in reducing STDs.

In 1981, encouraged by the progress of Deng Xiaoping's reforms and opening up of China, Hatem proposed a goal of eradicating leprosy in the country by the year 2000. He had already adopted a highly effective drug cocktail, but the three drugs were too costly, so during the 1980s, even as his health was failing, Hatem visited many countries to promote exchanges and cooperation between Chinese and foreign medical circles. China received medicines and equipment from leprosy foundations in many nations, including Japan, the United States, Italy, Belgium, Canada, the Netherlands, the United Kingdom, and the former West Germany. In 1985, in Guangzhou, Hatem held China's first International Leprosy Academic Exchange Conference. His war on leprosy won him many awards, including:

1979: Outstanding Service Award, University of North Carolina
1982: Damien-Dutton Leprosy Award (Belgium)
1985: California State Senate's Certificate of Achievement in International Public Health and Leprosy Prevention and Control
1986: National Order of the Cedar, Commander (Lebanon)
1986: Albert Rusk Medical Award (USA)
1986: Albert Lasker Public Service Award (USA)
1987: Honorary doctorate of science, State University of Buffalo, New York
1988: Gandhi International Leprosy Award (India)

Hatem died in 1988, leaving behind Sophie, their two children, and four grandchildren. Sophie died in 2023 at the age of 104.

In 2014, Ma Haide's life of love and service to China was told in the thirty-episode TV series, *History Will Always Remember* (历史永远铭记).

On September 26, 2021, the 111th anniversary of the birth of Ma Haide, the People's Medical Publishing House in Beijing published *Ma Haide the Great Doctor*, with over four-hundred thousand words and almost 180 photos recounting his life in China.

Dr. Haide's story was told in Edgar A. Porter's book *The People's Doctor*.

21st Century AI-Assisted Barefoot Doctors?

In 1977, China's barefoot doctors inspired the Thirtieth World Health Assembly's goal of "Health for All by the Year 2000," and the famous 1978 Declaration of Alma-Ata that asserted primary health care is a human right.

Sadly, by the time of Hatem's death in 1988, few politicians had done much more than spout slogans, but Harvard's Dr. Winnie (Chi-Man) Yip, Professor of the Practice of International Health Policy and Economics, suggests the answer to caring for the world's poor may lie in a twenty-first-century AI-assisted version of China's barefoot doctors. She wrote:

> The barefoot doctor program was a low-cost strategy that achieved high health outcomes. Its core principle was to keep people healthy. And the program reached everybody—it was universal health care in its very core. Just as impressive, barefoot doctors were part of the community, understood the community, cared about the community, and were trusted by the community.
>
> My idea of a twenty-first-century barefoot doctor is someone with two to three years of training post–junior high school, who will be enabled with artificial intelligence and big-data-assisted decision support. Apps or web-based tools will use data analytics to prompt the doctors to ask the right questions, supply the likelihood of various diagnoses, and recommend treatment. It's an algorithm decision tree but supported by big-data analysis.
>
> Twenty-first-century barefoot doctors will be most suitable in areas that are remote and rural and have older people left behind in the global wave of migration to cities. These doctors will need to be respected as the foundation of the health care system. They will also need to

> earn a decent income—although income alone is not what will keep them in their jobs. If twenty-first-century barefoot doctors become a reality, it could transform today's treatment-centric health care systems into systems that keep people healthy—and at scale.*

It's a vision that the American-born Lebanese-Chinese doctor Ma Haide would have been proud of.

* "Off the Cuff: 21st Century Barefoot Doctors," Harvard T. H, Chan School of Public Health, September 13, 2018, https://hsph.harvard.edu/global-health-population/news/off-the-cuff-barefoot-doctors/.

CHAPTER ELEVEN

The Team That Took on Hollywood

"Why should I, an A-level director, hire an unknown C team from China?" the HBO director asked Christopher Bremble, the founder and CEO of Base FX.

"Because my team guarantees A-level work," Chris replied.

The director still turned Chris down—but called him again late that night after watching the 2008 Beijing Olympics opening ceremony directed by acclaimed Chinese filmmaker Zhang Yimou. "He saw what Chinese were capable of!" Chris said.

Chris' fledgling media company not only landed the HBO project but went on to win the first Emmy for a media company in Asia. Today, the company has completed over 150 films, won three Emmys, and has been nominated twice for the Academy Awards for "Outstanding Special Effects," for *Captain America: The Winter Soldier* and *Star Wars: The Force Awakens.**

---

* "Our Story," Base Media, accessed January 18, 2026, https://www.base-fx.com/our-story/.

Base FX has offices in Beijing, Wuxi, Xiamen, Kuala Lumpur, and Los Angeles. I met with Chris in Xiamen, and after hearing his story, I said, "I could not tell your story as well as you do. Would you write it for me?"

Thank you, Chris, for telling us how your little team took on Hollywood.

Why China?

I was born in Ohio but grew up in small town north of Philadelphia. It was mostly farms, with a hospital and courthouse. I had, as a child and as a young man just out of graduate school, no interest in anything West of the Santa Monica pier in Los Angeles. I had never thought about China beyond my history books, and certainly never imagined living there.

But a man who owed me money called me one day and said I needed to go to China for a week and he'd pay what he owed me plus some more. I was a young and hungry screenwriter, so money of any kind was enticing.

I agreed and landed in Haikou shortly after midnight in August 2002 and drove through a humid city being constructed and de-constructed at the same time, buildings going up and coming down, workers pushing late into the night. It was like nothing I had ever seen or known, and I went to sleep that night unsettled by the energy and activity I had witnessed.

I woke up in the morning—not sure where I was—and opened the curtains of my hotel room to see a building across the street being demolished by several hundred workers. They each had a sledgehammer and were taking down the walls on every floor all at the same time. Tiles and bricks flying down, passing floors also being demolished. It was chaotic and magnificent. The pace, the effort, the shouting, and the perseverance—it was August in Haikou, and hot—were beyond belief.

It was in that moment that I began my journey to now.

I was a filmmaker, a writer, and understood the energy, passion, and commitment required to make a film. In my first few days in China, I met other filmmakers and young people who shared that passion. My first ever conversation in China, minutes after stepping off the plane, started with "Do you know Brad Pitt?" I didn't. But in the coming month Zhang Yimou's film, *Hero*, would be released, marking the beginning of the modern film era in China. And that energy, that drive I had first witnessed in Haikou made me want to participate and contribute in the moment, to witness and engage a budding film industry.

My next step in the journey was bringing a project to China, where I hoped to find a post-production company to work on the film's visual effects. This was in 2003, and there were no companies in China doing serious visual effects for films, but I found a school in Beijing teaching students how to use the Maya Cinemas app for visual effects and the teachers were eager to work on a Hollywood film. They gathered around me, looked at the storyboards, and declared they could do the work—all of it—as a team. Again, I was struck by the energy, the confidence, and the enthusiasm of the teachers—most of them still in their early twenties—to take on something that would be seen around the world.

We worked for a full year to deliver that first film. At the end of the process, I acquired the school. The teachers became the department leaders of my visual effects company. And in doing the impossible—more than three hundred shots on a tight budget with a young team—we set the culture for the company: there was nothing we couldn't do or learn to do well.

Our first project as a company was clearly an impossible task, but it was the only project that we could secure as a young company. The team worked around the clock; we bought cots so artists could sleep in shifts at their desks. We ate meals as a team, everyone together, sitting on the fire escape for lunch and dinner each day, then rushed back to the work. We didn't have enough computers—we didn't really know how to use the software well enough to avoid mistakes—but we had courage and spirit, and we had belief that we would be able to deliver on time. Everyone pushed to their maximum ability, our only focus the project's success.

The crew led by Chris Bremble that proved they could do "A-level work."

Out of that time came the nucleus of a company, and several families. Of the eight original members of the company, two were already married to each other and the other six married their team members. These four couples helped set the company's culture—to do the impossible and deliver it on time and beyond expectation. This culture was to be tested again and again.

Our big break came a year later, as the company was bidding for our first big American project, a high-profile film for HBO. The director of the project did not see why he should send work to China; it was a big budget show and there was no lack of money for quality work. I was informed we would likely not get the project. Then, later that night as I was sitting in the office, the distant sound of fireworks from the opening night ceremony of the Beijing Olympics barely audible, my phone rang; it was the director. He called to say that he was watching the opening ceremony on TV and couldn't believe his eyes. "I was so wrong," he said, "to say what I did today.... This is just incredible. I want you guys to work on the show!" I told the team: yes. We were all in the office, none of us watching the ceremony because there was work to be done, and everyone just went back to work. I've since had the opportunity to thank Zhang Yimou more than once for that moment—for showing the world the talent, effort, creativity, and ambition of China.

Yet another year later, in 2009, and our biggest opportunity arrived—the one which set our course as a business, and for, many of our staff, set the course for their careers. We had been working on the series *The Pacific*, for HBO (the first project had gone well). For most of our work at that time, our work was simple: clean up, wire removal, background mattes. Few clients in Hollywood trusted a small company in Beijing for anything more complex. I was in Los Angeles, delivering some of our work and meeting with the production team for visual effects, when the phone rang at the production office. The producers were not happy with the biggest sequence in the show and wanted it to be replaced. The sequence had taken a company in LA more than eight months to complete, and there were less than three months left to deliver the series for broadcast. While I listened to the visual effects team discuss their options, I took a chance. "We can do it," I said. They looked at me like I was crazy, but I had worked out the math, a plan, and a schedule in my head. "No," they said. It was too risky. They could lose their jobs. I volunteered that we would do the work for free. "Only pay us if you use it," I said. And to that, they agreed and arranged to send us the film plates. I went straight to the airport, buzzing with excitement—and fear, as an HBO executive called me on the phone: "Don't do this," he said. "You're doing well, becoming a trusted vendor. This is a high-profile show, and if you fail, that's it. We won't come back to you again for work." I held fast; I had every confidence in the team and knew this was a rare opportunity to show what we could achieve.

I arrived in Beijing and gathered the team, sharing the work, the opportunity, and the schedule. It felt—even to me, as I shared the details—more impossible than I had initially thought. The team pulled together a plan, and everyone confirmed it could be done, but everyone acknowledged it would be our biggest challenge. My job was to get practical effects to put into the shots—explosions big and small, smoke, bullet hits—so that we could save time and money. A few phone calls and three days later, a friend and I were at the August First Film Studio outside Beijing, filming as a pyrotechnic specialist made explosion after explosion. It was, looking back, one of the best filmmaking days of my life, working with the team at the studio to film challenging and critical elements. We finished the day exhausted, our ears ringing from a day of big blasts.

Over the next six weeks, the team worked on the sequence. At the time, the internet was at best challenging, and so the team would often divide up the materials for review with our partners in Los Angeles, and we would all go home to upload from our home internet accounts—the only way we could deliver the work on time to view. I have bittersweet memories of staying up all night to watch a file upload that would today take less than ten seconds. We had other challenges—our servers died mid-way through the project, forcing us to rework the entire project as the data was lost—but the work was delivered on time, the producers loved it, and we were paid well for the work. We had also proven ourselves to the visual effects team on the show, who almost immediately awarded us with more work, and also included us—me—in their awards nominations.

So, yet another year later, and I was sitting in the audience at the Creative Arts Emmy Awards, having been nominated for our work on *The Pacific*. I had zero expectations. When the visual effects award category came up, I started to text my wife that we lost, partly to push the disappointment out before it even arrived, when the person behind me lifted me up from my chair, shouting, "You won, you guys won!" I walked to the stage in disbelief, my phone still in hand, and by the time I reached the stage I had tears streaming from my eyes. They were tears of joy—not for myself, but for the forty-five artists back in Beijing who had worked tirelessly for months on the show, and now had won, for the first time for any studio in Asia, an Emmy for visual effects. Our little team, working out of a still active metalworks in central Beijing, sleeping on cots and sharing our meals, had won the second highest award in the industry. I flew home with the Emmy, and then spent what felt like days taking photos with the team, bringing the award to events to let the audience take photos with it. The award—to a small company in Chaoyang District—electrified the industry.

It also electrified the company. Within the next three years we would win two more Emmys, for *Boardwalk Empire* and *Black Sails*, and forge an alliance with Lucasfilm and Industrial Light & Magic, the leaders in the industry. I would meet—and secure investment—from the man who gave me my love of cinema, George Lucas, of *Star Wars* fame, and the company would be working on *Transformers*, *Pirates of the Caribbean*, and Marvel movies. Our young staff grew to almost 450 artists, with the best recruited to work around the world in London, Vancouver, New Zealand, and Australia. We worked with the biggest directors: Michael Bay, J.J. Abrams, Martin Scorsese, the Russo brothers.

Chris Bremble with Base FX's first Emmy, for *The Pacific*.

In China, as the industry exploded in 2012 with the success of *Lost in Thailand*, we built a client base of top directors, including Zhang Yimou, Lu Chuan, Chen Kaige, Guo Fan, Jiang Wen, and Raman Hui.

Our relationship with Raman and producer Bill Kong on the film *Monster Hunt* was a special relationship. I had met Bill through an old friend, and after showing him some of our work and having a long talk, he shared Raman's vision for *Monster* and asked if Base FX (my media company) would be able to do the work. *Monster* was, at the time in 2010, bigger than anything we had done. This time, the team joined me in reviewing the work and committing to take on the challenge, which would last nearly five years, until the film was released in 2015. As much as any other project before, *Monster Hunt* helped to define the studio, and in hindsight I can see how the team developed from its close work with Raman, an experienced and supremely talented animator who had become a talented and thoughtful director. The summer and fall of 2015 also marked, in some way, the high-water mark of our achievement as *Monster Hunt* and *Star Wars: The Force Awakens* hit theaters; both films broke records, won awards, and cemented the team's success. In the two years following, many of our best talents would leave for abroad, start their own companies, or move into directing or supervising for clients.

Telling Chinese Stories to the World

I had always feared what might happen once we had achieved our goals. By 2015, we were short only an Academy Award, though our work had been nominated for *The Force Awakens*. But as all of this was happening, we were also busy building something new—an IP business, focused on animation, to help tell Chinese stories to the world.

As we were closing our agreement with Lucasfilm in 2012, it was clear to me from seeing how an incredibly well-run services and IP company was run, that Base FX needed a larger "base" of revenue to survive. In 2013, with support from our partners, we began to invest in IP and plan for building an animation company. At that time, the talent available in China was too small to make even a single film at a global standard of quality, and so we focused on finding stories we believed in and thought would resonate. Our goal was to tell stories about China to the world; we wanted to be entertaining, not cultural or intellectual.

In early 2014, I came across a talented writer, Chris Appelhans, a character designer and concept artist for animated films. He was working on the idea of a story based on the Aladdin legend, but set in today's Shanghai. His approach to the story was personal; he had a close friend who lived in Shanghai who had shared his challenges coping with the pace of change and life priorities as China boomed economically. Chris showed me his illustration of a dragon in modern Shanghai with the title *Wish Dragon*—and that became the origin of the film. I began working with Chris and agreed that he write and direct the film. He had other offers for the project—from big Hollywood studios—but he was intrigued by Base FX, our commitment to our team in China, our ability to perform (we screened *Monster Hunt* for him), and my vision for the company.

It would take nearly seven years to get the film made; we ran out of money a few times, were rejected by all the Hollywood studios once, and some twice. In the end, we found partners in Sony, Tencent, and Jackie Chan's company, Sparkle Roll, with Jackie agreeing to star as the dragon in the Mandarin version of the film. We hired the best talents in Asia—mostly from China—and brought them all to Xiamen, where we had established a small office. The pre-production work was largely done in Los Angeles, but the production work—the acting and animating and lighting and magic—was done in Xiamen. It was an exciting time. We had also secured the participation of Aron Warner, an Oscar-winning animation producer, and with his guidance we dove into production.

We finished the film just a few days before the pandemic, in late January 2020. I recall leaving the wrap party receiving texts about something in Wuhan.

As the pandemic broke and the world stopped, so too did our plans to release the movie in the summer of 2020. As the months wore on, and hard decisions were made, Sony suggested we sell the film to Netflix. We agreed. In China, we committed to a release date in early January 2021, only for COVID-19 to break out across the country just days before, shutting down almost half of the nation's movie theaters. The film performed okay, lower than our expectations, and it was a bitter pill to see something we had put so much of ourselves into fail to reach a wide audience. For a time, I was crestfallen.

Then, as summer came, we prepared for the film's release on Netflix, on June 11, 2021. The film was released in China on my father's birthday and it was released to the world a day after my mother's, which—since I'm a somewhat superstitious person—gave me hope for its reception.

The story of *Wish Dragon* is that of a boy who, at the age of nineteen, feels that something in his life is missing. He longs for a reunion with his childhood friend, and when he is granted three wishes, it's this reunion that he wants. But the dragon says, "Stop! I can't do love . . . I can't make people fall in love with you." And so the boy must go about securing his wish without the help of magic wishes. He's tempted to take riches and power, but, in the end, he uses his last wish to save someone else. The story is set in today's Shanghai; the location for the boy's home was based on the home of one of the company's founders just off Huaihai Road. It's a story about values, and what's important.

The film, when released on Netflix, exceeded our expectations of how it would perform. It was in the top in ninety-one nations around the world and finished the year as the fourth most-watched film on Netflix for 2021. The marketing team shared that it was the most re-watched film on the platform, and continues to be until today, as more than two-hundred million people around the world have watched it, making the film the most watched film about contemporary China I know of. It's not a Wuxia (martial arts) film, or a historical film, but a movie about the challenges to life as we know it right now. Our research team discovered that audiences were struck by how similar our characters' lives were to their own, how similar their families and friendships were to those of people in London or Mexico City.

Promotional poster for *Wish Dragon*

This is what makes me most proud: We produced and shared a slice of the China we know, the China we live in, with the rest of the world. It was hard to make. We nearly didn't make it. But it stands as an accomplishment for the amazing artists who worked on it, pushed through weekends to hit quotas and stayed late to check on lighting adjustments. Production staff who reviewed and re-reviewed schedules and staffing profiles came in early to prepare for the day ahead.

Today, our teams of the past have spread across China and the world. The pandemic was challenging to an industry that relies on movie theaters being full. The company continues, and is preparing the sequel to *Wish Dragon*, which has an early scene in it that shows a building coming down all at once, a nod to that first night and day in China.

That first morning, waking to see those workers bringing down a building with their tools, has always been a guiding memory. My time in China has been marked by the ability of the young people I've worked with to push; by their belief in hard work as a path to a better future; and by the willingness to engage the moment and succeed. I've seen it in artists as they rise to become superstars in the film industry, and in young production coordinators who join the company, learn what it is to be professional, and go on to be successful managers across the industry. In my time in China, I've seen the past torn down, brick by brick, and a new China built to take its place. It's been a privilege to participate and to be witness to the moment.

CHAPTER TWELVE

Better Nearby Neighbors Than Distant Relatives*

When Paige Kuhn (程佩吉) moved from a small Wisconsin town of ten thousand people to Nantong, China, she quickly learned why Chinese have long said, "In times of need, a neighbor nearby is better than a relative far away." Or, as one Chinese said, "You can choose your neighbors, but not your relatives." But few are as fortunate as Paige to have a neighbor who became like a second mom, "always there, keeping an eye on me to make sure I was taken care of."

On a hot summer day in 2015, a couple of months after moving to China, Paige was returning to her apartment building

* This story is adapted with permission from Luz M. Sanchis, "15. Neighborly. By Paige Kuhn," June 1, 2022, https://www.mts-tech.com/2022/06/01/15-neighborly-by-paige-kuhn/.

during a class break when a woman standing on the stairwell shouted at her excitedly: *Méinǚ*! (美女, "beautiful girl"). Paige was already used to Chinese strangers waving at her and calling out, *Wàiguó rén*! ("foreigner"). Yelling "Foreigner!" is not at all considered impolite. The Chinese are merely stating the obvious—and usually with a smile of welcome.

Some Chinese, of course, are a little subtler about asking if you are a foreigner. A grizzled old farmer in a remote village once scratched his chin, smiled at me, and said, "Your hair is blonde, and you have blue eyes." He ponder this a few moments, then said, "You're not from around here, are you?"

So, Paige was well used to people yelling "Foreigner!" But no one had ever yelled, "Beautiful girl!" Had it been a man, Paige might have worried, but *méinǚ* is also said of children, and Paige was young, and pretty, though not quite a child. The Chinese woman kept waving and walking toward Paige, then said something in Chinese.

Paige had no idea what she was saying, and just shrugged her shoulders in what she hoped was a polite manner. Had it been a decade earlier, their conversation might have ended right there, but in an era when even remote Tibetans use phones for e-commerce, this tech-savvy lady was undeterred. She whipped out her phone and used a translation app to ask, "Are you an English teacher?" When Paige nodded, the lady motioned for her to scan her WeChat QR code. Paige scanned the code and politely bid her goodbye.

Paige did not expect to hear from the lady again. Chinese's daily exchange of WeChat is like "let's do lunch sometime" back in the US. It's usually just a polite way of saying, "Nice to meet you. Hope we meet again but it's not likely." But as soon as Paige reached her apartment she began receiving a string of rapid-fire messages. The first was brief, and in English, but then longer questions in Chinese followed. No sooner had she right-clicked for a translation and digested the question than she received the next one. "Are you in China alone? You are so brave. Do you cook? After we finish moving in we will be neighbors and you can come to our apartment for dinner!"

Taken Under Wing

As promised, Paige was invited for dinner as soon as the family had moved in. Over the course of several meals, Paige learned more about the lady and her husband, their second grade son, and the daughter who still lived with the grandparents in the countryside. Paige wrote, "She was outgoing, warm, and friendly, and I started to realize that she was taking me under her wing."

Paige Kuhn at the Great Wall.

Mothered and Doctored

Paige's neighbor became like family—and, not surprisingly, also like a family doctor.

Many foreigners are surprised to learn that Chinese greetings are often personal questions. Three decades ago, the most common greeting was, "Have you eaten?" but now that few Chinese go to bed hungry, they ask, "Going to work? Going shopping? How much did that cost?" And, like Westerners, many Chinese also ask, "How are you?" (*Ní hǎo*? 你好?). As in America, the usual reply is, "I'm fine, thank you. And you?" But unlike in America, if you even hint you are unwell, your Chinese friend won't let the matter rest until they've recommended you drink lots of water, rest, and take some exotic Chinese herbal medicine. And as Paige soon discovered, if you don't have Chinese medicines, your Chinese friends will buy them for you—and even brew them up if you are new at boiling elixirs concocted of sundry beetles, barks, herbs, and powders.

A week after Paige met her neighbor, she began to feel ill while teaching. By the time she got home, she had a fever, was vomiting and had to run to the bathroom every five minutes.

Paige was miserable. "I was away from home, still very new to China, and was at a loss as to how to take care of myself. Everything was in a language I couldn't understand and unrecognizable. The medicine was foreign, the hospital system was foreign, the foods were foreign. Having planned to stop by my neighbor's that day, I sent her a message to let her know I wouldn't be coming because I was sick."

Paige's neighbor immediately replied that she'd visit as soon as she got home from work.

"No need, thank you," Paige replied. "I'm okay for tonight." So, the neighbor waited until the next morning, then messaged,

"I bought you some medicine last night, but it was too late to bring it to you. Are you home?"

As soon as Paige set her phone down, a knock came at the door. Her neighbor was carrying a bag filled with boxes and boxes of medicine. Using the translation app, her neighbor typed, "I have some medicine that is good for your stomach. It will stop the nausea."

Some foreigners, myself included, balk at taking herbal medicines prescribed by a Chinese neighbor or friend who really has no idea what's wrong with you other than that you are *bù shūfu* ("not well"). They'll swear that the shopping bag full of medicines they've just purchased will fix you up. I've even had students in my classes notice I seem tired, and they'll hand me a bottle of tiny black pills resembling rat pellets, made from poisonous toad venom (no joke!) and say, "This will help!" Yet to my surprise, their medicines almost always do help, perhaps because they tackle the general "not well" problems—the nausea, diarrhea, headaches, fever, fatigue. After all, the world's most populous nation has had thousands of years to find cures for *bù shūfu*. Even better, Chinese have for at least two thousand years emphasized preventing disease over curing it, so your neighbors will show up on your doorstep certain days of the year with special foods or tonics that will fortify you for the new season approaching.

Paige's neighbor strode confidently into the kitchen as if she owned the place, brewed up a concoction of dried pellets, and told her to drink it to calm her stomach. She then waltzed out the door and returned shortly with a lunch tray of rice, fruit, and green veggies. Paige said, "My stomach churned at the thought of eating much of anything. Grateful, though, I accepted the tray and ate what I could."

Paige survived, but her neighbor continued to care for her. Paige became like a daughter to her and was even invited to join the Chinese family during their October first to seventh National Day holiday on a Yangtze River boat trip. When Paige's family visited not long afterwards, her neighbor drove two hours to pick them up from the airport, treat them to dinner and take them to the most popular tourist and cultural sites.

Paige's neighbor took them to visit a famous water town nearby, and her mom wandered the rows of shops, browsing the quilts that the town was famous for. Her mom wanted to buy one of the quilts but to the shopkeeper's frustration, Paige's neighbor kept saying, "I can get you a better buy." The unhappy shopkeeper yelled at them as they walked away.

Paige's parents returned to the US, but the neighbor had not forgotten the quilt.

Leaving the Nest

Paige's neighbor watched over her carefully, making sure the "brave single girl" from abroad was taken care of, but just as Paige neared the end of her one-year teaching contract, she met the man whom she would marry, and the neighbor could see that Paige was "leaving the nest." Her contacts became less frequent up through the time Paige moved to another Chinese city to be with her husband—but Paige had yet to hear the last of her adopted mother.

Paige wrote, "Several months after I moved away, I made plans to visit my family in the USA for Christmas. My neighbor had found out about my travel plans just days before my departure and hurriedly overnighted me a package. Even while living in another city, my Nantong neighbor wouldn't let me go without a gift of kindness. Remembering our day at the water town, she had shipped a brand new, beautiful quilt for me to carry back to my mom."

Like many other Americans in China, Paige had learned that a neighbor nearby beats a relative faraway—and once a neighbor, always a neighbor, no matter how far one travels.

CHAPTER THIRTEEN

Mea Andrews

Finding a Home in China

Mea Andrews moved to China in 2017 "to better my writing by experiencing new words, places, and people," but to her dismay, her new life did not broaden her perspective but narrowed it—at least at first.*

She chose Asia for her new life, and chose China not because of its rich history or culture but simply because it had a lower cost of living than Japan or South Korea. She was given a choice of Chengdu or Shanghai. Many would have chosen the futuristic "Pearl of the Orient," but Mea states she "chose Chengdu because of the pandas." But just as she was setting

* Luz M. Sanchis, "14. My Time in China: Redefining Home by Mea Andrews," May 26, 2022, https://www.mts-tech.com/2022/05/26/14-my-time-in-china-redefining-home-by-mea-andrews/.

out, the company messaged, "Well, actually now you must go to Chongqing."

No pandas for Mea, but in retrospect, it was *Yuánfèn* ("fate"). When asked about the change of plans, Mea said, "So while Chongqing wasn't where I chose to be, I did really enjoy the slightly more relaxed lifestyle there and, looking back, I much prefer Chongqing over Beijing, Chengdu, or Shanghai now that I've spent time in these places. It was accidentally a great fit!"

But China was not her cup of tea at first.

Chongqing was worlds apart from her hometown of McDonough, Georgia. Founded in 1823, McDonough had 29,051 people as of the 2020 census. Chongqing, by contrast, was first settled over two thousand years before the US was a gleam in George Washington's eye, and has a population of thirty-two million over an area of 82,400 square km (the size of Austria, half the size of Georgia).

Mea quickly found that "experiencing new words, places, and people" was far easier in theory than practice. She had expected to share her new life through her poetry, and she did enjoy the spicy Sichuan cuisine and hotpot, and "incredible mountain views that rival Hong Kong." But though she loved the place, the people were another matter.

Not one for attention, she did not care for being treated like a pseudo-celebrity. Every time she walked out her door, she got what nineteenth century foreigners called "The China Stare." She was especially annoyed by everyone taking her photo, though endless photos did not bother her foreign colleagues. She said, "Now, about six years later, I can firmly say I absolutely dislike the 'celebrity status.' Taking photos with strangers means I need to try to look acceptable all the time and being stared at is something I have tried to get used to and just can't.... I'm not that interesting; I haven't done anything to deserve that level of attention, so it feels very strange to me."

But she soon discovered just how novel and interesting she was in Chinese eyes when a lady in Henan asked if she could get the COVID-19 vaccine when Chinese and foreigners had different blood and internal organs. It was hard to realize just how "alien" people seemed to think she was.

As Mea's frustration grew, her poetry reflected her negativity. She shared with the Macon Writers Group in 2023:

> Living in Chongqing, I experienced a series of cultural clashes that led me to write unflattering poetry about the society I was immersed in. I panicked; this wasn't the work I wanted to be producing. Somewhere along the way, I lost sight of experiencing another way of life to broaden my own way of thinking and instead used it to become even more narrow-minded.... How could I express my experience living abroad from my point of view in a fair and just manner?*

Mea's predicament was of course far from unique. Judgmentalism, often rooted in a sense of superiority, is universal, and even worse when it happens across cultures or races.

Fortunately for Mea, she recognized she was unfairly judging China. She said, "There are plenty of truly lovely people in China. Setting things up in China takes a lot of effort and there was always someone around willing to help me get a SIM card, download apps needed to survive in China, get me to the

---

* Mea Andrews, "Writing Across Cultures," *Macon Writers Group* (blog), June 1, 2023, https://maconwriters.com/f/writing-across-cultures.

hospital, etc. It's a bit of a trade-off: being more noticed also means people are a bit more understanding that I might struggle to do something."

Mea Andrews traveling in her newfound home.

Removing Mea from the Picture

As Mea began to better appreciate those around her, she tried to be less judgmental and more objective in her poetry, and found inspiration in early-twentieth-century Russian writers. In 1910, Acmeism made its debut with Mikhail Kuzmin's essay, "On Beautiful Clarity." Acmeism embraced conciseness, clarity, and "direction expression through images" rather than confusing symbolism.*

* *Who's Who in Twentieth Century World Poetry*, eds. Alan Parker and Mark Willhardt (Routledge, 2002), 8.

Symbolist poets or painters rely upon a shared history, culture, or mythology to share their message, but symbolism fails when author and audience are from different worlds. Mea decided to attempt "direct expression" by taking herself out of the picture and just writing what she saw without judging or explaining it. Mea said,

> I started writing what I saw without pushing myself into the scene more than necessary. I dropped all symbolic gestures, instead choosing the event as it happened, minus my opinion or thoughts. To observe more, I started writing about others' interactions with each other rather than their interactions with me. In some cases, I simply wrote about places I visited.
>
> With this new method of writing, I was able to see the universal traits that connect us all instead of focusing on the negative things that specifically weighed on me. I was able to connect with people on a more personal level, and surprisingly, I was able to let go of past experiences in my life that had influenced my writing up until that point. Going abroad had finally done what I had wanted it to do automatically when I stepped off the plane, it had made me able to think more easily from other's points of view.... All I had to do was remove "me" from the scene and instead focus on what was happening around me.*

With her newfound appreciation of China, Mea found that one year was not long enough. She signed on for another year,

---

* Andrews, "Writing Across Cultures."

promising herself, "I'll leave after the third year." But by then, China was in her blood. Mea shared, "There was no way I could just leave all of these great people behind, so I stayed another year...and then COVID hit, and right in the middle of that, I got married."*

Marrying Across Cultures

It's no surprise that Mea met her future husband online, given that China has the world's largest internet network and the most active netizens. They first met on Tantan ("Explore," 探探), the popular Chinese dating app now used worldwide. A year later, Mea came across the same guy on Tinder and messaged, "I know you!" They began dating soon after, and a year later were married.

Wedding day, Chongqing

Marriage is challenging, and cross-cultural marriages more so, but marriage during a pandemic was an epic challenge. Mea said, "Of course, marriage is never easy, but it has an extra twist when it includes what can be exasperating cultural differences and trying to get acquainted with a new family."

* Sanchis, "Mea Andrews."

Mea found that she and her husband even expressed affection differently. Her husband showed his love through actions; while she preferred words (not surprising for a wordsmith). It was tough some days but now she says, "It took some time [for us] to push past that, but it's all good now. We tend to meet each other in the middle these days."

Mea at the 2022 Paralympic Games with her husband.

Her new Chinese family had understandable qualms about their new foreign daughter-in-law. "There were concerns that as a foreigner, I would run away back to my country, or that I wouldn't have much in terms of family values and would simply choose divorce if times got tough.... But despite that, my husband's immediate family was incredibly welcoming of me."

Chongqing to Beijing

After their wedding, Mea and her husband discussed where to live: a) Stay near his sisters in Chongqing; b) Move closer to his parents in his Henan hometown; or c) Get her husband a green card and return to the US. They eventually chose d) "None of the above."

Chongqing was beautiful but they had already seen much of it and were ready to move on. Neither had ever lived in a tier-one city, so they chose Beijing—but only temporarily. Mea said, "Our life in China looks very much open-ended, we know we want to go to Guilin, Guangzhou, Xi'an, and so many other places in the near future."

Mea's China journey did not start well but she's grateful she stuck it out. She now appreciates and even respects the differences between Chinese and American cultures. And to her amusement, her husband has also changed. She still does not like strangers taking her photo, and neither does her husband.

At first, he had accepted the staring as normal, but when he speaks English with Mea in public, many Chinese stare and ask where he's from. Mea mentions, "It was novel at first, but now we can gripe about it together on particularly bad days." But most days she's grateful for experiences that friends back in the US would never dream of. She said:

Where I'm from in Georgia (though technically I grew up shuffling around the majority of the southern states), many people never have the opportunity to travel abroad, much less live in another country for a long period of time. China has given me the ability to grow in ways I had not expected and will be my home for years to come. I suspect China will always hold a special place in my heart.

Back in the Picture

In 2022, Mea was one of two recipients of the *Door Is a Jar* literary magazine's 2022 award for poetry and fiction that "use language in a way that alludes to emotions or events larger than what's contained in their pages."

This seems to me like the symbolism Mea once avoided, but perhaps she now knows both worlds well enough to put herself back in the picture.

But I won't ask to take her photo.

CHAPTER FOURTEEN

Becoming "Rachel in China"

I did not realize I'd begun to take China life for granted until I began reading blogs such as *Rachel Meets China*, by a young American from Texas. Her enthusiasm and sense of wonder reminds me of myself three decades ago when I happily lugged around a massive camera and an eight-pound videocam to capture everything from old men playing checkers and a bike repairman brewing tea to the granny who led her flock of goats over the Xiamen University hills every morning to sell us milk fresh from the source.

I may have arrived in China decades before Rachel, but I'd like to follow in her footsteps and travel China again to see it from her fresh and unfettered perspective.

Greek to Me

As a teen, Rachel knew nothing of China except what she'd learned from Disney's *Mulan* film, but while studying public relations and communications in college, she met many Chinese students who happily shared with her what life was like back in China. She had no idea that China had such a diversity of cultures, minorities, foods, and music. Yet as intriguing as China sounded, she'd have probably never considered a trip to China had she not first spent a semester studying in Greece.

Only about half of American adults own passports, and eleven percent have never even left their home state.* But Rachel's semester in Greece was enough to hook her on foreign travel. She determined to go abroad for a year as an English teacher, and where better than China—especially given the many companies that help young American college grads attain TEFL (Teaching English as a Foreign Language) certification and jobs.

In 2015, Rachel moved with four other young Americans from her university to Hunan University in Hengyang, Hunan, to teach sophomore and freshman English. She told friends and family she'd return to real life in America after one year; she's still in China eight years later.

It's obvious that Rachel has been in China awhile when she catches herself calling Hengyang a "small town." Hunan's second largest city, Hengyang has over seven million people—small by Chinese standards, perhaps, but almost one quarter of the population of Rachel's home state of Texas (the largest state, area-wise, of the forty-eight contiguous states).

Rachel was almost clueless about China. She could not speak Chinese or read Chinese signs, and it was hard to find English speakers in such a "small town". And like many foreigners, she was surprised that people stared and wanted photos with her. But

* Lea Lane, "Percentage of Americans Who Never Traveled Beyond the State Where They Were Born? A Surprise," *Forbes*, May 2, 2019, https://www.forbes.com/sites/lealane/2019/05/02/percentage-of-americans-who-never-traveled-beyond-the-state-where-they-were-born-a-surprise/?sh=fa10ef289848.

unlike others, Rachel did not mind the staring and the photos, and embraced the people's uninhibited friendliness.

Rachel later shared her gratitude that she had started out in a small town rather than a modern city. The inconvenient transportation, and the lack of an expat community and Western restaurants forced Rachel to "embrace and enjoy the local Chinese experience"—and she embraced life in China with a passion.

Rachel was delighted to discover that Hunan boasted a rich culture and history. Hunan was Mao Zedong's hometown, and home not just to Chinese but also such minorities as the Miao and Tujia, who are famous for such unique practices as the "weeping weddings." Rachel also discovered that the *Avatar* movie was filmed in Hunan's otherworldly Zhangjiajie National Park.

Rachel especially enjoyed Hunan food—once she'd mastered chopsticks well enough to get it to her mouth. She discovered that Chinese food in China was different from Texas' deep-fried American Chinese food slathered in sweet and sour and lemon sauces. Rachel sampled everything from duck's blood to pig ears, cow intestines, and donkey meat.

And Rachel quickly learned to say, "Less spice!"

Although Sichuan is famous for spicy fare, many Chinese claim Hunan food is even hotter. But Rachel slowly came to love the flavor bombs. Like Hunanese through the centuries, she found the fiery fare not only helped her cool down during the summer but also keep warm in the winter.

Rachel also enjoyed getting with students and friends to make *jiaozi* (Chinese dumplings), which archaeologists have discovered have changed very little for almost two-thousand years.

Rachel grew to appreciate the sharp clack of tiles while playing Mahjong, practicing the slow-moving martial art Taiji, and dancing with Chinese women in park squares. She also sang lots and lots of karaoke—which may be where she first fell in love with Chinese popstar Zhang Jie.

In September 2015, just after she'd moved to Hunan, she attended a university Mid-Autumn Festival party. As the lights dimmed and a freshman group began to dance, she heard "the voice of an angel" through the speakers. Rachel had no idea what he was saying but she loved his voice.

Rachel decided to learn the song herself, found the lyrics in pinyin (the phonetic symbols for Chinese characters), and practiced it on her Chinese friends. They applauded, in spite of her poor pronunciation. Chinese, of course, are so appreciative of people learning their language that they'll compliment you even if, like me, you spend your first few weeks in China greeting them with "How's your horse?" (*ní máhǎo*, 你马好) instead of "How are you?" (*níhǎo ma*, 你好吗?).

Rachel discovered that Zhang Jie's English name was Jason, he could sing in English, and in 2014 he had won the "Best International Artist" award at the 42nd American Music Awards. She also found that her idol was married to a beautiful Hunan TV host named Xie Na. "They were married in [Yunnan's] Shangri-la (heaven on earth) and I'm only a little jealous."

Rachel's students humored her Jason obsession and brought her Zhang Jie gifts—postcards, photos, books, a pillow with his face on it. Years later, her Hunan students still message her whenever they hear news about Zhang Jie, and when his wife had twins, one messaged, "Rachel, you have become a stepmother today!"

Many of Rachel's students were from rural areas and had never seen a foreigner. She enjoyed her students so much that she often had them over to her small apartment for "hotpot parties," to learn American games such as Uno, or to play the students' childhood games.

After a year in Hunan, Rachel had barely scratched the surface of life in China, so she stayed a second year, and then agreed to teach English to kindergarteners in Guangzhou, a diverse city that has been an international port for most of the past two-thousand years. But although Rachel loved teaching, after three years she decided to capitalize upon her PR and communications skills and took a digital marketing and media job in Beijing.

Rachel had visited Beijing but never imagined living there. Yet she discovered China's capital was a "perfect mixture of traditional culture and modern life. It's so different living in Beijing than being a tourist in Beijing.... I loved Beijing, my job, my friends, and the community I built here, and couldn't imagine leaving."*

Even after settling down in Beijing, Rachel continued traveling. She loves the diversity across China, from large cities to rural villages, and each place's unique dialect, customs, and foods. "So even though you're still in China, when you travel it's almost like traveling to a new country. It's changed my life in so many ways!"

Rachel Meets China Travel Blog

A born communicator, almost from day one in China, Rachel began sharing with family and friends back home her life and experiences on her *Rachel Meets China* travel blog and on Instagram. But the more she traveled in over twenty-four provinces, and the more she learned, the keener she became to share with a wider

---

* "My Journey: Rachel Meets China," Wellcee, accessed May 7, 2025, https://www.wellcee.com/article/my-journey-rachel-meets-china?id=1600337744576272 4.

audience and to encourage others to visit and explore China. She expanded her content from simple tourism to helping other expats who found life in China intimidating because of language or cultural barriers. She even co-created the popular *Date Night China* podcast, and after eight months, began dating the co-host. Friends joked, "If you can't get a date, start a dating podcast!"

Rachel's content has become so popular that she is frequently interviewed by the media or other content creators. Tourism companies ask to partner with her and various brands seek her help.

In 2021, Rachel found an even broader outlet for her communication and PR skills when she accepted a position as a video host with CGTN's English channel, China Plus. Although Rachel's CGTN documentaries, vlogs, and livestreams about Chinese culture and travel reach a far larger audience than she could have imagined, there are pros and cons. She feels much freer on her own, filming herself with a tripod and gimbal. But with a professional team, she need not worry about technical issues and she has recorded scenes she could have never captured on her own.

But Rachel never imagined such videos could get her branded as a tool of the Chinese government.

Enemy Influencer?

In July 2021, Rachel was shocked when Facebook and Instagram labeled her private accounts as China state media, even though she had been posting only her own personal content since 2015. The same month that Rachel's content was targeted, BBC posted an article, "The Foreigners in China's Disinformation Drive."*

* Kerry Allen and Sophie Williams, "The Foreigners in China's Disinformation

Rachel's content, however, had never been political, but focused on promoting understanding and awareness by posting personal experiences about people, places, and culture. "My account is always my voice," she wrote, whether she is creating for her own blog or China Plus.

Rachel mentioned Andy Boreham's December 2021 article about "the West's push to ban good news about China online," which warned the world about foreigners who dared paint "cheery portraits of life as foreigners in China."* Boreham summarized their verdict: "Any positive news about China must be fake, funded by the Communist Party of China, and therefore should be labeled as 'misinformation.'"

Rachel has yet to resolve the China media labeling but she presses forward, cheerful and grateful for her eight years of experiences that have given her a greater appreciation for both China and her own home:

> China has totally turned my world and perspective upside down. Life here is brilliant and bizarre and at times challenging, and it's filled with incredible travel adventures and the most amazing people. I love sharing about life in China and write posts all about teaching ESL in China, tips for living abroad, guides for traveling, special experiences and events in China, and also just day-to-day life here. . . .

Drive," BBC, July 10, 2021, https://www.bbc.com/news/world-asia-china-57780023.

* Andy Boreham, "Your Life in Shanghai Sucks, Okay?!: The West's Push to Ban Good News about China Online," Shine, December 18, 2021, https://www.shine.cn/opinion/2112179662/.

. . . If you want to step outside your comfort zone, go skydiving. If you want to forget you ever had a comfort zone, buy a ticket to China.

CHAPTER FIFTEEN

"Little Monkey" Gracie's China Childhood

"You should move to Xiamen!" I urged Sam Burgess for the dozenth time. "The city is beautiful, universities pay better, they'll stick to the contract, and living conditions are far better." But Sam always refused in spite of the many challenges.

"I agree a bigger city has more advantages," Sam said. "But it's too hard for Putian to find foreign teachers, so I'll stay for now."

They stayed eighteen years, and their love for their "second home" rubbed off on their children.

In 2012, young Sarah Burgess emailed me to ask, "Uncle Bill, would you like to write a book about Putian with me?" She'd been taking notes and photos and was ready to tell the world about the wonders of Putian, but I didn't think Putian had that much to write about. In fact, when I wrote the book, *Fujian Adventure*, I did not include a Putian chapter because I thought it had nothing but the Southern Shaolin Monastery and Meizhou Island's Mazu sea goddess temple. But when I said that within earshot of little Sammy Burgess, he let me know that he too was proud of Putian and it had a lot to see!

The Burgess kids cycled around town with me, pointing out old architecture and regaling me with tales of old Putian. They proudly showed me ceramic shards they'd dug up by an ancient stone home that once had two turrets, like a castle. Putian was settled in 568 CE, and I was surprised to learn it was only seventy-two miles from Taizhong, Taiwan, where I lived in the 1970s. I visited the beautiful Nine Carp Falls, and the "dream praying temple" where people sleep overnight to dream answers to problems. Putian is also famous for its over twenty varieties of lychee fruit. The famous poet Guo Moruo wrote, "No place in Putian is without lychee trees." Putian people love the fruit so much that they even stir-fry it.

I learned that Americans had been in remote Putian well over a century when the Burgess family led me on a hike through the forested hills to show me the well-preserved grave of Fred Lincoln Guthrie. An American missionary born in Jacksonville, Illinois, in 1865, he helped start an orphanage, nursing home and St. Luke Hospital (now the Affiliated Hospital of Putian University) and was principal of the Hinghua Anglo-Chinese School. On the day after Christmas in 1904, he raced to the hospital carrying an unconscious Chinese boy. Medical staff saved the child, but Guthrie died of a heart attack.

As I learned more about Putian, I saw why Sarah was so excited about writing a book about her second home. Her passion inspired me to learn more about the ancient city, and if I ever rewrite *Fujian Adventure*, I'll add a Putian chapter—or maybe two.

After eighteen years in Putian, during which Sam Burgess's

wife, Cathy, was given Fujian Province's Friendship Award, the Burgess family reluctantly returned to the US in 2020—but I had not heard the last of them. On Mid-Autumn Festival 2023, I was delighted to receive an audio WeChat message from Sarah's younger sister, Gracie, with holiday greetings in fluent Chinese. She said, "I'm finally back in China, after almost four years! I'm working for a Guangzhou company that has a warehouse in the US. They sent me here for a month to get to know the company better, and help see what position I can fill in the future. I was excited to tell you that I'm in China too now!"

When Gracie said she was making a quick trip to visit her old friends in Putian, I said, "Would you be willing to share your China story? I watched you grow up in Putian for eighteen years."

Gracie was surprised. "Sarah and I were just talking about writing our story!" she wrote.

I look forward to reading Sarah and Gracie's China story, but for now, here's Gracie's tale.

Gracie "Little Monkey" Burgess in Putian

I was on a business trip to China when our old family friend, Uncle Bill, asked me if I was interested in writing some of my story and I could not say yes more quickly! I had not expected to be away from China for three years and was so glad to be back. So, where to begin my story, my love for China and all the things that have happened there?

My family moved from Texas to China in 2002 when I was five years old. None of us could speak Chinese or had much knowledge of the culture or ways of China. We had not even eaten Chinese food. But my parents had made a trip to China to visit orphanages and fallen in love with the Chinese people, and they wanted to somehow make an impact and contribute to China.

Young Gracie Samson

My dad had initially thought of moving his software company to China, but a Chinese exchange student living at our home told us about a small coastal city in China called Putian. Putian had one university and they had a hard time getting foreign teachers because it was, by Chinese standards, a "small city," though with 3.2 million people, its population was sixteen-times larger than that of Chattanooga, Tennessee, where my parents had met in university.

The Chinese exchange student gave us Chinese lessons, and we tried our best to learn—well, the rest of the family did. I'm not sure about myself. I was apparently very stubborn and the only Chinese word I became fluent in was *xi gua* ("watermelon"). Very useful, right? Who would have guessed then that Chinese would become almost second nature to me?

When we first arrived in Putian, it had one traffic light and one KFC. And I remember learning to use chopsticks at the same time as I learned to use a Chinese brush for calligraphy. I got the two confused and to this day, although my Chinese is fluent, I still hold my chopsticks incorrectly. I think it keeps me humble.

I don't remember that much about our first year there, as I was so young. But I do remember lots of mosquitoes and the high humidity, and I loved the tropical fruit growing right outside our building. But speaking of our building, it was the only place that I really remember feeling like home. Let me tell you about it.

I grew up on the first floor of building 36, *Dao De Lou* ("The virtue building," 道德楼), where the university hosted all foreign teachers. Since our family had seven people, we were given two adjacent apartments, 101 and 102. We had gatherings in apartment 101 because it had a very large wooden table, which they'd moved from the school library because it was the biggest table they could find and the only table all seven of us could all fit around (I am the youngest of five; my siblings were fifteen, thirteen, twelve, and nine). Apartment 101 also had a kitchen and two toaster ovens, the school room, and two bedrooms, which we all shared. Apartment 102 had our grand piano, "dad's office," and two other bedrooms. Over the years we five kids hopped around from one room to another, and I am pretty sure I lived in almost every room except my parents'.

My father taught computer science and my mother taught English, but also somehow managed to homeschool all of us—except for me during the years I was in Chinese school.

There was not a moment where our home did not have visitors, and these visitors quickly became like family to us. We loved to have students over for parties where we taught them games like charades. I remember students always being at our house for Thanksgiving, Christmas, and all the other holidays.

One of our biggest challenges each year was getting the turkey for Thanksgiving. When we first moved to China, we were taken care of by our dear friend Mr. Wang. He had once been an exchange student in Texas and experienced American hospitality during the holidays. He became a very good family friend and through the years introduced us to more friends, including the mayor of Putian. Each year, we would host a big Thanksgiving party for students and friends. Once, even the mayor and his wife attended.

At that time, it was a huge ordeal, and we would spend up to three days preparing traditional Thanksgiving food for our friends—and Mr. Wang was the one who helped us find the turkey! I remember getting into the back of a small van with an American teacher and one of my sisters and riding to the countryside. The van stopped on a random side street and we got out. The driver opened a door to what looked like an empty storage room and when we peered inside, guess what we saw? Three turkeys—one big Tom Turkey and two smaller ones. The driver asked us to pick one. I was too upset to pick one, but our friend pointed at one of the smaller ones and, well, the rest was history. My mom was delighted and surprised when she was presented with a full-sized turkey and had to cut the legs off in order to fit it in our small toaster oven.

China Schooled

Since I was the youngest, my parents thought it would be best to send me to the local kindergarten so that I could learn the language. I couldn't really understand anything for the first six months, but after that I slowly started to catch on. I remember mimicking what my classmates said until the words started making sense to me.

After kindergarten, I studied at a local primary school. I was the only American student and my classmates welcomed me with open arms. I quickly became one of them. I was even top of the class and got an award for being "Most Like Lei Feng," a young soldier in the 1950s who Chinese hold as a role model. I proudly wore my red scarf and tried to join the socialist youth committee. I was a bit disappointed when I found out it was only for locals.

Gracie with her grade school teacher and a friend.

In so many ways, my childhood was just like my Chinese classmates—except when my English teacher would ask me to lead the class in our daily reading. I remember my parents strictly warning me not to correct her English pronunciation.

Like other Chinese elementary students, I stayed up late doing homework and woke up early to ride on my brother's bicycle to school. Elementary school laid the foundation for my language knowledge and I am forever grateful to my parents, my teachers, and my classmates for being there for me.

I have so many fond memories of growing up in China. I always knew it was lunch time when I could hear our neighbor's wok sizzling with oil and the metal spatula scraping against it, or the vegetable lady calling out in the local dialect, right outside my window, "Come buy vegetables!"

Gracie with guests at her big Thanksgiving gathering.

From sixth through twelfth grade, I was homeschooled because I also had to learn Western courses to prepare for university, which I thought would be in the US but turned out to be in Taiwan and Xiamen. I continued to live with my parents and make trips back to America during the summers to visit my grandparents. Since I was the last child still living at home when my parents decided to get their master's degrees in Hong Kong, I moved with them to Hong Kong for two years.

It was in Hong Kong that I began my search for universities and became intrigued with the idea of learning more of the Chinese language. I had spent most of my life translating for my parents and friends, and had developed a passion for helping others better understand each other.

I started school in Taiwan as a translation and interpretation studies major and after two years transferred to Xiamen University to study business Chinese.

In October 2023, I was finally able to visit Putian after a long three-year absence. I was filled with emotion when I walked up to our old apartment door and saw the old milk box still there. It still had the green metal doors with the faces of lions protecting us from danger, and the large tree that was in the center of the apartment courtyard. I remember that was one of the first trees I had ever climbed. I loved it so much that I was nicknamed "little monkey." It was under that tree that I huddled with the neighbor children to hear my first Chinese ghost story, and under that tree that I walked Peanut, our little Chihuahua. And it was under that tree that I learned to speak the Putian dialect from the vegetable lady.

To be honest, the past three years have not been exactly what I thought they would be. I never thought I would be away for so long. But this trip back was a beautiful gift, and a reminder to me of how much I love my home, China. I am not quite sure what the future will look like for me, but I know that it will definitely have China in it. I am looking forward to that, and I hope that more and more people can see the beauty, the warmth, the wonder of China, and most of all the Chinese people.

CHAPTER SIXTEEN

Mr. John M. Godwin

No Culture Shock in China!

"Most Xiamen International School (XIS) board members did not speak English," John said, "and I did not speak Chinese—but it was the best board I've worked with!" That was quite a statement from a man with fifty years of international education under his belt. John added, "And in China, I never had culture shock! Other countries, yes—but not China. Xiamen is my second home!" And he proudly showed me his "key to the city" that Xiamen's mayor gave him when he was named an honorary citizen.

Most Americans never go abroad, and of those who do, few make such an impact on their adopted communities as John Godwin. But John was not the first educator to fall in love with the island city known for centuries as "Amoy."

Even in the sixteenth century, foreign writers wrote of Amoy's deep natural harbor and, more importantly, the people's unparalleled openness and hospitality. South Fujian (Minnan) had for centuries been the start of the ancient maritime silk road, which inspired Xi's modern Belt and Road Initiative. Minnan people had traveled abroad and welcomed merchants from all over the known world, and by the early twentieth century, Xiamen's Gulangyu Islet International Settlement was called the "richest square mile on earth." Gulangyu was also one of the most talented square miles on earth, thanks to twenty-plus educational institutes that produced leaders in every field from music, arts, and literature to astronomy, medicine, and sports.

John Godwin speaks at Xiamen International School.

But when I moved to Xiamen in 1988, I saw few hints of its former glory. It seemed like a backwater, and even its designation as a Special Economic Zone in 1980 did not seem to help much. Few foreigners moved to Xiamen, and most relocated after a year or two to larger Chinese cities with better healthcare and education for their families. But Xiamen Mayor Hong Yongshi helped turn things around in the 1990s with his two-prong strategy: world class medical care, and Xiamen International School

(XIS). Today, Xiamen is once again a hot destination for both Chinese and foreigners—but XIS had a bumpy start.

Xiamen had high hopes for XIS when it opened in 1997 with eighty-one students, many of them the children of parents working at Kodak's largest facility outside of New York. In 2000, our governor, Xi Jinping, who had been Xiamen vice mayor over a decade earlier, visited XIS and praised the school's role in Xiamen's rapid growth. But from day one, XIS leaders found that creating a close-knit team from diverse and strong-willed expat educators was harder than herding cats. So, Xiamen's leadership cast their net far and wide to find an academic leader who could put XIS on firmer footing—and John Godwin was their godsend.

With three degrees in education and communication, and experience across the globe, John was certainly qualified to tackle XIS's challenges. But what won Xiamen people's hearts even more than John's credentials was his personality. His infectious laughter—and beard—reminded me of Burl Ives, the famous mid-twentieth-century folk singer. There are probably few headmasters on the planet who can tackle serious issues with parents in the morning and in the afternoon dress as Santa Claus to hand out gifts to students.

John Godwin transforms from headmaster to Santa Claus.

John not only forged a tight, professional, loyal, and dedicated team of faculty and staff but also helped energize parents, and even give the K-12 students a love and pride for their school and their city. But how did John end up in Xiamen, and why does he call Xiamen his second home? We're grateful to John for telling his story of fifty years in international education in his own words.

Reflections On An International Career, by John M. Godwin

It was only in my junior year of university that I made a final decision to become a teacher. I had briefly worked as an elementary teacher's aide at a school and enjoyed it tremendously. My goal was a career in which I could find both enjoyment and fulfillment. I had already had a number of temporary jobs, which helped direct me away from going into a career that offered only financial satisfaction.

After being a public school educator for fifteen years in Southern California, the "international travel bug" bit me. California was becoming far too crowded and I began feeling more like a bureaucrat than a teacher. I decided to interview with DoDDS (Department of Defense Dependents Schools). It was a great interview, and I almost wound up going with DoDDS. But the interviewer happened to tell me that International Schools Services (ISS) was also recruiting. Well, that was enough for me!

I quickly signed up for the 1989 ISS recruiting fair in Los Angeles. It was my first fair and my head was spinning as I went through a whirlwind weekend. I received a number of offers. Admittedly, I was a bit nervous and puzzled about what to choose, but I met some wonderful people. Whether they had been in the system for years or only a short time, they all talked about how wonderful it was! That was exactly the push I needed.

Like many folks at the time, I initially thought I wanted to go to Europe, but that wasn't what life had in store for me! I surprised myself by making my first adventure in Saudi Arabia. I wasn't sure what to expect, but it turned out to be so much more than I could have thought. Besides being at a wonderful school doing what I loved to do, I was able to travel Saudi in my car. I drove across the desert, up along the Red Sea, further to Amman, Jordan where I left my car for a weekend, crossed over into Israel by bus, and was let off in Jerusalem. I explored old Jerusalem, which was wonderful, but one of my highlights was completely accidental. I took a taxi to Bethlehem and learned that Bishop Desmond Tutu was speaking to a group of Palestinians on Christmas Eve. Afterwards, I was invited to a Palestinian home for tea and cookies. They simply wanted to tell me their stories, like the Intifada (Palestinian Uprising, 1987–1993). Completely unexpected!

The next year, in Saudi Arabia, by virtue of being the school's representative to the American Business Association, I was invited to a luncheon with General Norman Schwarzkopf and his junior officers just prior to the first Gulf War. Having come from a military background, the luncheon and discussions were very comfortable for me.

As I moved on to other postings in other countries, I had many fascinating adventures. I loved my work at the International School Manila, enjoyed the great beaches, snorkeling and diving, and marveled at the warmheartedness and kindness of the Filipino people.

The next posting, however, to Vienna International School, brought a new meaning to adventure. I met Geri McMahon, and after six months of dating, we had our required official civil marriage ceremony. It was all in the German language, as was our marriage license. We had some wrangling over German-to-English translations, as we both speak, read, and write just enough German to get us into difficulties.

We invited the entire school to our celebration at a *Heuriger* (wine tavern) in the Vienna Woods—and most of them showed up! The fine Vienna wines flowed almost as heavily as the Danube throughout the day, night, and into the early morning hours of the next day.

My next two international postings were again in Europe (Germany and Poland). I loved driving a car and riding trains throughout Europe, and in Vienna I had learned to ski, so I often took ski vacations with my wife Geri and son Matthew.

One of my most memorable highlights in Poland was being invited to share a Shabbat meal with a rabbi and the American consul general in Krakow. As I learned the meaning of the event, I was deeply touched and wavered between tears of sorrow and joy at being able to share in it.

One of the board members in Poland was chatting with me over coffee one day about his business in Xiamen, China. He said he was really impressed with a small school there named Xiamen International School. He said, "If you ever have the chance, that would be a great place to work and live; and the international school is excellent."

My next posting was a short interim position back to Germany, but when I saw an opening that year for XIS, I applied. A few months later, I was invited to XIS to interview. It was a wonderful little school and still in the early stages of its development, and I was delighted to be chosen as its next headmaster.

It was a pleasure watching XIS slowly grow and develop over a period of years. And, as usual, my wife, son and I would also manage to go on vacations in China (Beijing, Xian, Yangshuo County, and others) and nearby countries in Southeast Asia (Vietnam, Cambodia, and Thailand), some of which were beach vacations, but certainly not all. We also managed to travel to the North Island of New Zealand where we rented a car and saw the sights of that island on our own.

No career, however, would ever be complete without some time in Mexico. I had a little more of my travel-thirst quenched by some time spent in Monterrey, a large industrial city in the north central region of Mexico and not far from the Texas border. Once again, the school was exceptional and the school community was wonderful! And we had some incredible vacations. The people and culture of Mexico will always be dear to me, as I had lived near the border for many years. But my thoughts kept going back to Xiamen.

I decided to end my fifty-year career with a final excitement in Xiamen, China, which had become my second home. The school community was second to none. The board, in my humble opinion, was the best board I ever worked with. Mr. Deng and Dr. Hu, the two board chairs, were always working with me to improve the school. There were never any hidden personal agendas and we had the same goals. We listened carefully to each other. Their support, as well as the staff's and the city's, made living and working in Xiamen the acme of my career. The deputy head, David Wei, and the personnel director, David Huang, became my good friends and a most vital help to me with both school improvement and government relations. Meeting and getting to know Dr. Bill Brown, a founder of the school, and his family was another highlight of my time in Xiamen. They had already made Xiamen their home. They helped me come to see the Chinese people for their warmth, friendliness, and kindness.

The city of Xiamen fits the term of being the smallest big city I've ever lived in, although, by Chinese standards, it was relatively small, at almost five million people! When I returned to XIS, the school's population had doubled in size from my first tenure and had undergone tremendous change that one only sees by having been at a school for a while. My ten wonderful years at XIS were the best educational and cultural experience I ever had. I am so grateful for the opportunity to have lived, worked and ended my career in Xiamen, China.

I am also grateful to life for having taught me that in this wonderful and grand international school circuit, what matters most is not what we are given but what we give. Yes, I know, it's a cliché to hear, "'Tis better to give than receive." The reality, however, is that it's the truth. That is truly what brings the greatest joy, the greatest satisfaction. The rest is just a little icing on the cake.

One last thought to reflect upon in these current times, and so very well stated long ago, is by American writer Mark Twain in his novel *The Innocents Abroad*:

> Travel is fatal to prejudice, bigotry, and narrow-mindedness, and many of our people need it sorely on these accounts. Broad, wholesome, charitable views of men and things cannot be acquired by vegetating in one little corner of the earth all one's lifetime.

CHAPTER SEVENTEEN

A Texan Luthier's China Dream

A Beijing guitarist was shocked when I pulled both a computer and my guitar from a twenty-two-inch-long bag. "Better than a rabbit from a magic hat!" I said. "World's best collapsible, full-sound guitar—designed and made in Xiamen. I can't carry my full-size guitar on a plane but this fits in the overhead."

The guitarist smiled, but said a bit smugly, "People know me. I can always carry my guitar on a plane."

Nice to be famous, I thought. But five days later, he messaged me. "Where did you get that guitar? Today, I could not carry my guitar onboard!"

The innovative Texan founder and CEO of Journey Instruments and Convergent Sourcing, Rob Bailey, had no interest in China as a youth—except for Wing Chun kung fu (咏春拳), which he studied in his Austin, Texas high school. "I was a big fan of Bruce Lee, Jackie Chan—all the great kung fu guys."

In addition to kung fu, Rob loved languages. At the University of Texas (UT), Austin, he studied Spanish, French, classical

Greek—but no Chinese.

It took an epic romantic misadventure to get Rob to China.

While majoring in philosophy and preparing for his wedding, Rob's life was turned on its head when his fiancée fell in love with his roommate. "I was kind of at a loss," Rob said. "I did not know what I would do."

"Kill your roommate?" I suggested.

To add insult to injury, Rob's dorm contract forced him to share his room for six more months while his ex-fiancée and roommate dated. "It was so painful," Rob said. So, a friend said, "Hey, you should do a foreign exchange program in China—kind of clear your head, have the experience. Kind of reset your life."

"Sounds like a great idea," Rob said. In the summer of 1996, twenty-two-year-old Rob took a summer program at Hebei University of Science and Technology. "I loved it!" Rob said. "I loved the people—so friendly—and the food was so good, and I had a good Chinese teacher. That was my first time ever studying Chinese. I was kind of a natural at it, and I just loved it."

But Rob discovered that Chinese and Americans have very different teaching styles. "It was funny," Rob said, "we had this teacher who in class was like a Nazi—*so* strict. She was, like, crazy, like, traditional—*hen xiong* ("so fierce")! But outside of class, we went on a field trip, and she was like a bubbling little girl. And all the guys were wondering, "Who are you?! How is this possible?"

Their teacher said, "Well, you know, in China, in class, you have to be strict—but outside of class we can be friendly!" Rob said, "She was not what I expected of a Chinese teacher. But it ended up we all just loved her, and we all did great, and that's where I got the Chinese name *Luomin*—*Luo* for Robert and *Min* for my middle name."

After just two months in Hebei, China was in Rob's blood. He returned to UT to finish his undergrad degree in philosophy and classical Greek literature, then signed up for a two-year program at another university of science and technology in China, this time in beautiful Hangzhou. "And I just loved it, I loved it. It was great because my teachers were really good—all my teachers were Chinese." But the honeymoon ended after the first semester.

Rob's classmates in the first semester were all Americans, so it was fairly easy for a guy gifted in languages to stand out. But every classmate in his second semester was Asian. "I was the only non-Asian, and I thought it was so unfair because it was so much easier for them. I studied ten to twelve hours a day just to keep up—but it helped because within two years I was pretty fluent. But then I had to decide what to do next—grad school in Texas or accept one of the job opportunities from China's Mainland or Hong Kong?"

A coin flip decided Rob's future. "I'm young, I thought, I don't know what I'm going to do, so I'll flip a coin. Heads, graduate school in the US; tails, Hong Kong. It was tails, so I moved to Hong Kong—and that's where I met my wife, Emily."

Rob recalls that when he first met Emily, a Chinese woman from Hong Kong, they had no interest in each other. "We weren't attracted to each other at all." But one day at an activity with youth at a Spanish tapas restaurant, he was impressed by how she spent time counseling young girls with personal problems. Rob said, "I saw her love for the other girls. Some people, you know, enter a room to just network, and use other people as tools. But some really delight in other people, and when I saw how Emily cared for others, at that moment I really fell in love with her. And I thought, *I gotta pursue this woman!*"

Emily had spent eight years studying in the US, including

at Andover prep school and Brown University. Founded in 1778, Andover was the alma mater of people like the two Bush presidents, five Nobel Laureates, and Facebook founder Mark Zuckerburg. For 2022 to 2023, the acceptance rate was only eleven percent. And Brown University, founded in 1764, accepted only 5.2% of applicants. This was one smart girl, and beautiful—but it was her heart that really got Rob's attention.

Rob told Emily he'd like to date her—not just casually, but to see if perhaps they might someday get married. Rob said, "Her response was—she just freaked. She kind of just dropped her jaw. She was silent for what felt forever, though it was probably just ten seconds. And then she said, 'Let me think about it.'"

"How long do you need?" Rob asked.

"Anywhere from one week to five months," she replied.

"That was a looong time! But I said, 'Alright.' She called in about a week and said, 'Let's talk at a park.'"

"For Western guys," Rob said, "when a girl says she wants to talk at a park, that usually means she's gonna turn you down, so I brought my gym clothes to Hong Kong's Victoria Park so afterwards I could work out and burn off steam from the rejection. But when I walked into the park, she said, 'Let's give it a shot!' And then my jaw dropped! I didn't know what to do. I didn't have any plans after that."

Instead of the gym, they talked at a coffee shop, and Rob dated Emily for about a year and a half until his job contract ended and he felt it was time to return to Texas—but without Emily!

While Rob worked for a Taiwanese tech company in the US, Emily had been accepted for programs in social work at Colombia University, University of Chicago, and UT. Rob had considered UT for an MBA or studying law, so when his company offered to pay his MBA tuition if he stayed with them, he agreed.

Emily also chose UT, they continued dating, and got married.

In 2006, Rob and Emily moved to Xiamen, where he helped a Texas company start a sourcing arm. They had different management philosophies, so Rob bought out the company and turned it around. "The good thing is," Rob said, "we worked it out and we're all still good friends."

It was perfect timing for a company like Convergent Sourcing, which linked Chinese firms with those in the US and Europe. Rob's full-service operation streamlined the value chain and not only helped assure quality products at competitive prices but also emphasized ethics in all aspects—especially care of workers. Customers, such as the famous American firm Precious Moments, appreciated that Convergent Sourcing inspected every factory to ensure working conditions were safe and that workers were treated fairly, avoiding practices like overtime without pay or work for weeks or months without a break.

"But how did you get from sourcing to collapsible guitars?" I asked.

"I played guitar all through high school and college," Rob said, "and about 2010, I bought a carbon fiber guitar to carry on consulting trips." Carbon fiber is ten times stronger than steel and impervious to temperature or humidity changes, but even so, it was hard for Rob to lug a full-size guitar on consulting trips—so he set out to solve the problem.

"I had two Chinese mechanical engineers on staff. One specialized in carbon fiber, plastics, and steel; the other did ergonomic designs for everything from medical equipment to home furniture. Those two men are my friends to this day." Rob helped them find work and let them use his office in return for ten hours each of engineering work per week. But Rob thought, *Hey, why am I using these two resources to make other people really profitable? Why don't I see what we can do together? And that's when I came up with the collapsible guitar. Why don't we see if we can do something in carbon fiber or wood? So, we did it!*

Rob thought up the designs, then the engineers turned the dream into reality by putting them on paper in a way they could be produced. "We worked together," Rob said, "and still work together. But I should probably learn CAD software on my own."

It took about a year and a half for our research and development team to develop a full-sound guitar with a removable neck that fit in a twenty-two-inch bag. They took the computer to the big NAMM (National Association of Music Merchants) trade show, and his friend James helped with the booth.

Rob's career path to becoming a luthier in China was not straightforward before he found success.

Rob now has twelve patents in China, the US, and Europe, and Journey Instruments's guitars are so popular that he struggles to keep up with demand—and also with musicians' rising expectations. Rob said, "Today's requirements are much higher than ten years ago. Guitarists really want perfection. It's very challenging—and it's probably not just our industry, but for a handmade product like ours, it's really a lot of work to do."

Fortunately for Journey Instruments, Rob's Chinese luthiers are excellent—some of them even trained under world-renowned Canadian luthier Jean Larrivée, who started out as an auto mechanic but began handcrafting in his basement the guitars now prized around the world.

Rob's innovative collapsible guitar is great for travel.

Rob's Chinese luthiers not only worked closely in making the guitars but also in improving and streamlining the development process. "It was hard at first and took a year or so to work out the bugs," Rob said. "But now the process is great. We still make small, incremental improvements, but the basic design hasn't changed. One carbon fiber factory said I was the only customer who has been producing the same design for ten years. 'We like to work with you!'"

Rob is especially grateful for his Chinese team. "Some of my staff have been with me for thirteen years. Turnover is really low—not perfect, but we're like a family. I can now manage much of it remotely, and I'm really thankful."

Although Journey began with acoustic guitars and expanded to classical, bass guitar, and now electric guitars and electric bass, the small electronic components such as guitar headphones amplifiers and guitar pickups that Rob designed have become popular, easier to make, and more profitable.

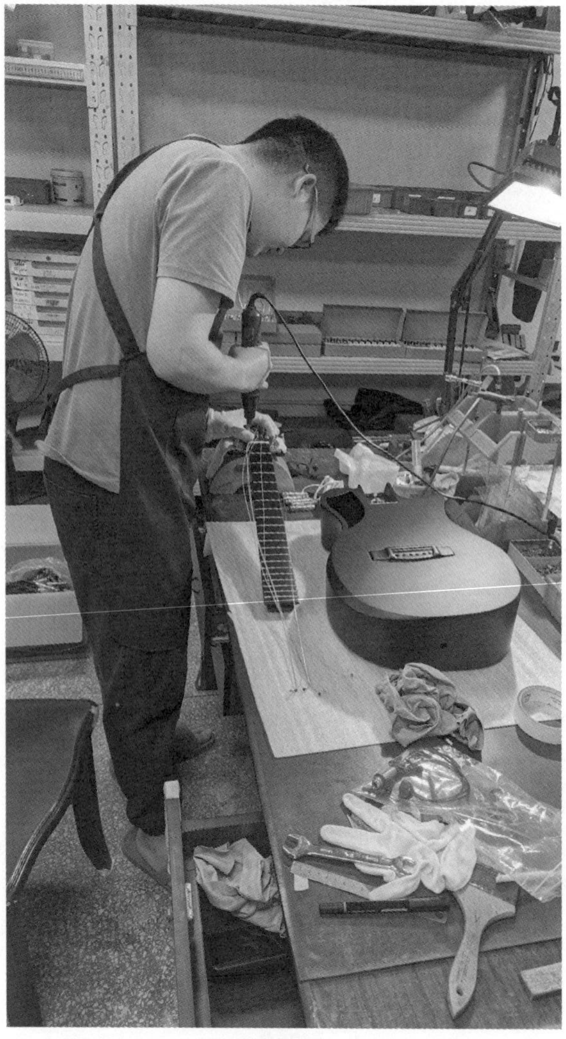

A luthier working for Rob makes a guitar.

Life in China

Rob had originally thought of doing business not in Xiamen but in Hangzhou, where he had gone to university, because larger cities have more opportunities for trade and networking. But Xiamen had more trade than he expected, a beautiful living environment, and it was only one hour by plane, or four hours by bullet train, to Emily's family in Hong Kong. Rob said, "I really enjoy living in Xiamen. We've loved raising a family here. Our oldest son loved going to the public Chinese school and made a lot of good friends. Our daughter went to the local Chinese kindergarten. We've enjoyed living here, and we've enjoyed the kids going to school here."

I also learned that at least one of the three kids shares Rob's love of kung fu. While at the Journey Instruments office, I saw one had just received a black belt.

The entire family also loves Chinese cuisine from across the country. "Cantonese is very delicate but flavorful, and I like Sichuan and Dongbei. And my favorite food in China is Yunnan—the perfect balance of a variety of flavors and spice!"

But Rob's favorite part of China is the Chinese themselves. "We've always enjoyed just the average Chinese *lao baixing* ("ordinary people"). I feel like the factory worker or the small shop owner or even the guy who sweeps the street—these people really are the salt of the earth. I feel like those people are just like the guy down my street in America. They genuinely care about people around them, and they're hard-working. Those are the people that make China great."

"The only reason we just moved back to Texas," Rob said, "and I go back and forth now is because of the kids' education. But I've always felt really at home in Xiamen. Even me coming back for this trip, it's kind of weird. I feel like I'm going to leave and feel torn again. Xiamen's a great place. I've loved the work and the life here."

Rob shows off his wares with author Bill Brown.

China has been a great business education, Rob says. "I feel like living here has given me a business sense that I would not have gotten in the States, or it would have taken decades longer to figure out. And the speed of everything here is so fast that I feel like the US is kind of slow in comparison—perhaps with the exception of places like Silicon Valley.

But Rob has some concerns about the US and China. "I feel like we're at a strange time in history. People in the US and China want to blame each other for problems, but my hope is that the US and China will have a healthy friendship. I hope that we can come in and out and continue to do business. Plus, these people in Xiamen who work for me—I want to make sure I have a good exit strategy for business. I want to make sure they are taken care of. I hope to see China pull through all these challenges."

CHAPTER EIGHTEEN

Davina Harden

China Chose Me!

"I really loved Xiamen," said Davina, an International Baccalaureate (IB) Program Coordinator of a school in Guangzhou. "I lived there six and a half years."

"If you loved Xiamen so much, why move to Guangzhou?" I asked.

She laughed. "The Xiamen school schedule clashed with my wedding plans, and I wasn't letting anything interfere with my wedding. But the Guangzhou school did not start until September."

Although she now teaches in Guangzhou, she still keeps a home in Xiamen because of her husband Cody's businesses—and so they can go enjoy the best of both cities.

This reminded me of the Ming Dynasty (1368–1644) tale of the young girl torn between two suitors—the rich but homely man from the East and the handsome but poor man from the West. She sighed heavily as she told her mother, "If only I could eat in the East and sleep in the West."

Although Davina said she would never live anywhere but China, her original goal was the Middle East.

"Were you interested in Middle Eastern culture?" I asked.

"No!" Davina said, "I liked it because it was tax-free. But I could not find a position I liked, and all my contacts kept pointing to China—so China chose me."

The oldest of three children, Davina was born and raised in Northern California and Las Vegas. "I knew nothing about Chinese culture or history," Davina said, "except that the Great Wall was cool. Americans don't learn about China in school, and we don't talk about it, so I had no interest in it."

But with part-Filipino ancestry, Davina was familiar with Asian cultures. Her ancestors had moved to Hawaii, and then to Northern California. Fully forty percent of Chinese Americans live in California, many of them the descendants of over forty-thousand Chinese who immigrated around the time of the California Gold Rush (1848–1855), and another fifteen thousand who arrived between 1863 and 1869 to work on the transcontinental railroad and later help establish California's agricultural and fishing industries. By 1880, according to the census, 12.14 percent of California's population was Chinese (and five percent today).

In 1905, Chinese were some of the earliest settlers in a remote train town named Las Vegas. Today, Vegas' percentage of Chinese is still small but their influence belies their numbers. And Chinatown Vegas, only five miles from the strip of casinos, is three-plus miles of Asian supermarkets, Chinese massage spas, martial arts schools, over 150 Chinese restaurants—even a dozen Buddhist temples and another dozen Chinese churches. Vegas was as close to China as Davina could get without leaving Nevada.

Davina especially loved Chinese food, although in China she discovered Chinese don't serve fortune cookies at meals, and her favorite Vegas Chinese dishes were not authentic—even when prepared by chefs who were straight from China and could not speak English. "There are two reasons for this," Davina said. "First, buying some Chinese seasonings in the US is as hard as finding some American ingredients in China [although Taobao now has everything imaginable]. And second, they had to adapt to Americans tastes."

"Canadians are the same," I said. "In Toronto, only Chinese would eat my friend's authentic Chinese cuisine, so he started slathering everything in sweet and sour and lemon sauces—and the media raved about his restaurant."

In spite of Davina's multicultural ancestry and exposure to Asian cultures, she never considered going abroad until she was finishing her first MA and was told by an academic counselor, "You'd do well overseas."

"He planted the seed," Davina said. But she must have been hard soil because it took six months before she started searching online for overseas learning or teaching experiences. She had two interviews in the US, and contacted many placement agencies, but was dismayed at the quality and costs of the services. "Some charged $200 just to upload my resume on their website," Davina said. But then she came across a placement agency that walked her through every step, from interview to actual placement—and all for free!

Davina was captivated by the description of Xiamen International School and its island city. She signed on for a year—and stayed for six and a half years because, "It was even more beautiful than they described."

She started with elementary students and then taught second grade, fifth grade, and became the entire school's reading specialist. Davina found that teaching in the XIS IB Program was much like teaching in an American IB program—especially at the elementary level. Children from countries across the planet thrived in the cross-cultural atmosphere, and although English was a challenge for some younger students, they improved rapidly.

"I loved teaching at XIS," Davina said. "I also enjoy my work as IB curriculum coordinator at the Guangzhou international, but it's not quite the same."

Davina missed XIS's strong school culture, but as I shared with her, it took years for John Godwin to help shape it. But Davina's Guangzhou school is still relatively new. Davina said, "It was a challenge creating a culture for my staff, which it did not really have yet. It was harder to get morale up and get them to trust that I'd do what I say. But it's the middle of the school year now, and teachers are coming around and starting to feel more like a collaborative team."

Davina also misses Xiamen city, though by keeping a home there she can return often.

Davina Harden enjoying a toast with her friends in Guangzhou.

"Guangzhou is very big," Davina said, "but also very traditional. It has pockets of Westerners here and there, but it doesn't really have the same welcoming feel of Xiamen, where the expat community is bigger. There's no sense of community in Guangzhou. Shanghai is nice, of course. It's more Western and has a much bigger expat community than even Xiamen, but Shanghai is too big and too fast—nonstop—and the people are not as welcoming as Xiamen people."

"What makes Xiamen so welcoming?" I asked her. I was surprised to learn that Xiamen's Chinese neighbors and coworkers played a larger role than fellow expats in making her feel at home.

Davina said, "The Chinese were such a help making me transition into the culture and way of life. I was the only foreigner in my neighborhood and spoke no Chinese. But my Chinese neighbors were always so helpful. I did not even have to ask for help. If they saw I had problems, or seemed concerned about anything, they were always there ready to help in any way they could—whether it was how to pay a light bill or order online from Taobao."

"How did you communicate since you could not speak Chinese?"

Davina held up her cellphone. "The Chinese did not mind at all speaking into the translator. They were not afraid or intimidated by such new technology."

I laughed at the thought of Chinese being intimidated by tech. Although we had no phones thirty-five years ago, and it cost me $450 USD and three years to get my first landline, by 2000, even monastery monks had cellphones. In January 2020, BBC boasted in the article, "How Covid Turbocharged the QR Revolution," that some UK restaurants and shops were using QR codes to accept mobile payments. The article even described how a phone could be used to scan a QR code. The article did not mention China, where beggars had been accepting donations with QR codes for a decade, and today, remote Tibetan farmers use their phones to buy and sell, and herders in Inner Mongolia track their sheep and cattle with cell phones and the BeiDou Navigation Satellite System.

One of Davina's greatest helps was her *ayi* ("helper," "maid"). Davina was hesitant to hire a maid because she thought she could do everything herself, and she also felt awkward about having a "servant." But like many Americans in China, she discovered that the everyday things can take all day to do. And as Davina's mother said, "Don't look at it as hiring a maid, but as giving back to the culture by giving someone a good job, and taking care of that person."

A selfie!

As it turned out, Davina's maid took care of her. "She was a lot more than just someone to cook or clean up," Davina said. "When I was sick, she'd ask me, 'Have you eaten? You have to eat something!'"

"I'll eat later," Davina told the maid, who promptly ignored her, made some soup, pushed her to eat a bit, and then put the rest on the stove and gestured for her to heat it up when she could eat more."

Davina said. "She could not speak English, but she just took charge and did whatever was needed. And sometimes English isn't needed—just a smile or a nod."

Davina traveling in her second home.

Davina's experiences with Chinese neighbors, colleagues, and even her maid reinforce the importance of Chinese who don't speak English reaching out to newcomers. Expats also play a role, as do organizations like Xiamen's official Guanren International Community, but ordinary Chinese reaching out in simple ways can help newcomers feel at home in China, rather than let them hide out in an expat cultural oasis (Chinese of course do the same thing in the US).

Davina especially appreciated the XIS Chinese coworker who helped explain the similarities and differences between Chinese and American culture. "She was just herself, "Davina said, "not pushing her culture, but if I had questions, she'd answer them all." And as Davina learned that there was more to China than the "cool Great Wall," she began exploring different parts of China.

Davina has traveled across much of China, but one of her most memorable experiences was visiting the Terracotta Army in Xi'an and buying a book signed by the "discoverer" of the sculptures. And Davina's most life-changing experience was the secretive "ice cream" at the Harbin ice sculptures to the far north on the border of Russia.

Davina's travels took her to see the Terracotta Army in Xi'an, one of the most inspiring sights she has experienced.

Davina visited Harbin with a Chinese girlfriend and Cody, an American who had lived in China for four years and whom she'd been dating. Before the trip, Cody asked her to map out an itinerary of sites she wanted to see. She jotted down the Siberian tiger sanctuary, a music festival, and saved the famous ice sculpture festival for the last day.

As the three wandered about admiring the ice sculptures, Davina's friend said, "We should eat some ice cream."

"Ice cream?" Davina said. "We just came from the canteen, and I don't want to go back. Besides, it's freezing! We need something warm." Her friend kept going on about ice cream, which she later found out was a code word between her and Cody, who said, "Let's get ice cream after visiting that ice bridge."

Davina walked under the beautifully lit ice bridge, strutting as if she were a model, then turned about and was shocked to see Cody on his knees holding up a ring. "Ice cream" had been their code for the perfect spot to propose marriage.

"What? Are you serious?" Davina began crying tears of joy.

So how did Cody end up in China? Like many other Americans in China, it was *Yuánfèn* ("fate"). While in the US, Cody had received an email that read, "Interested in China? Come teach!" Cody was a marketer, not a teacher, but he was curious about China and took an extended leave to visit. He discovered that teaching was not his cup of tea, but he loved China, so started a consulting business. When I asked Davina if they had any plans to return to the US, she said, "'No—China is home. Both Guangzhou and Xiamen!"

CHAPTER NINETEEN

Life in China—Everything, Everywhere, All at Once!

Ana thought she'd have to put her passion for volunteering on hold when she retired and joined her husband in China, but she's done far more volunteering in China than she did back in Texas. Ana laughed as she said, "Life in China is like being in a movie—everything, everywhere, all at once!"

Ana had been traveling to China for over twenty years because of her husband Tom's stone business. She stayed only a few weeks each time, but it was enough for her to fall in love with the country. She said, "Those brief visits allowed me to discover the beauty of China. Walking on the Bund in Shanghai at 6:00 in the morning, and seeing Shanghai *rén* ["people"] practicing tai chi, and dancing and singing—because Chinese love to dance and sing. You feel you are part of a movie. The Great Wall makes you think of the great people that lived a long time ago, but their presence is still here, for us to marvel at their legacy."

Ana's husband, Tom, has been in the stone business for forty years. He began buying and inspecting stone in China in 1999 but did not visit Xiamen until 2002. He was shocked at the size of Fujian's thousand-year-old stone industry. Tom had been to Carrara, Italy, the "marble capital of the world," where Romans were quarrying over two thousand years ago. But Tom said, "Xiamen was a thousand times bigger and the stone factories were working two and three shifts. It was an impressive scene."

Tom admired Minnan stonemasons' craftsmanship and creativity. Granite homes and pagodas along Fujian's coast have stood for centuries, and locals used to believe that only gods could have lifted the twenty-five-ton granite blocks for the nine-hundred-year-old, two-thousand-meter Anping Bridge. Ancient stonemasons even used bioengineering, with live oyster secretions to hold together the one-thousand-year-old Luoyang Bridge's massive stones. And Minnan stonemasons are the best in China to this day. In 1959, Beijing built the massive Great Hall of the People in only ten months because it relied upon Minnan stonemasons.

In 2006, Tom finally gave up his globe-trotting and focused on China as his base. He said, "China is dynamic, a 'Can-Do Country.'" He started Chuang Hong ("Everlasting Success") Stone, and his confidence in Chinese craftsmen paid off. CHS's clients include such companies as Hilton, Marriot, Shell, Exxon, and American Airlines, and its diverse projects have included the US Embassy in Rangoon, the Oklahoma State Capital, San

Francisco's McNay Art Museum, San Antonio International Airport, and many projects at top US universities.

But although Tom was happy with CHS, his wife had some qualms about moving to China long-term. "I was very excited," Ana said, "but to tell the truth, also a bit scared. It was one thing to be a tourist, but to settle down full-time?"

She loved the garden island's beauty. "To say that Xiamen is a pretty city is an understatement," Ana said. "Everything in Xiamen is beautiful—the city, the lake, the parks, flowers, coffee and tea shops. It is considered China's most livable city, and it really is."

But after a few weeks, Ana was growing restless—until she read an article about volunteer opportunities with the Guanren Community.

China's "neighborhood communities" meet many needs in society, but it is a challenge for them to help foreigners who don't understand Chinese. So, in the 1980s, the Guanren Community Center was established to give a sense of community to newcomers, whether foreigners or Chinese from other parts of China. The center helps residents with everything from finding a hospital, dentist, lawyer, or travel agent to renting an apartment or taking classes in Chinese language, history, arts and crafts, martial arts—even Chinese cooking. They also offer fire safety and life-saving demonstrations, and regular seminars on visa and travel guidelines or other subjects geared to expats. A favorite with foreigners is the monthly charity bazaar, with proceeds going to families or schools in need, or for relief of disasters such as the 2015 earthquake in Nepal.

The Guanren Community made Ana's life much easier and far more exciting. But more importantly, Guanren helped give Ana a new sense of purpose.

Ana teaching English at Guanren.

Ana was delighted to learn that Chinese also have a passion for volunteering—everything from giving free legal advice and medical care to planting trees, cleaning up marine environments, tutoring rural children, and reaching out to retirees and shut-ins. Even children volunteer. A teen studying English at night with New Channel Education said her family was not rich, but they were better off than rural students, so she spends two nights each week online tutoring rural children in math. It was gratifying to learn that even the rural children had computers and reliable high-speed internet.

As soon as Ana read about the Guanren Community, she asked if she could help with any projects. They asked her, "Would you like to give a conference on US culture next week to elementary school students to help them better understand foreign countries?" Ana's first thought was, *I am an accountant, and I've never given any kind of conference to schoolchildren.* But to her own surprise, she replied, "Yes, I can do it."

Ana spoke no Chinese, and the children spoke little English, but the Guanren team provided an interpreter and dropped them off at the school. Ana said, "I loved the reception that the school's teachers and students gave us. I was out of my comfort zone, and challenged, but loved every minute of it." Ana was delighted by the children's attentiveness and keen interest in everything she shared—and they didn't want her to stop! "They wanted more!" Ana said.

Ana enjoys her time with her students.

Ana also volunteered to teach English to migrant workers' children, and then spent four days volunteering in a small rural village a few hours north. "The goal," Ana said, "was to introduce rural children to other cultures, to open their eyes to different ways of living. It was a great experience and great adventure. I felt a real Xiamen *rén*."

On November 15, 2023, Ana received a special certificate honoring her leadership as the foreign captain of twenty-eight charity and education volunteer projects, having accumulated 138 hours of volunteer service over five years.

Ana and Tom at the Great Wall.

One of Ana's most fascinating activities was visiting a Traditional Chinese Medicine (TCM) hospital, where she saw doctors and nurses practicing such ancient procedures as acupuncture and cupping. Ana learned that Chinese and Western medicines have very different philosophies. Whereas Western medicine has until recently focused mainly on cures, Chinese medicine has always emphasized prevention. Even two thousand years ago, Chinese medicine emphasized a healthy lifestyle with proper nutrition (which varied for each season), exercise, and stress reduction, and paid doctors not to cure them but to keep them well.

Now that Tom's company has such capable leadership, he has been spending more time traveling with Ana to better understand their adopted home. Ana said, "The opportunities to experience China as a traveler are endless. And cultural differences can be interesting, shocking, even funny—and sometimes all at the same time!"

Tom and Ana have explored virtually the entire country. They've hiked the Great Wall, bicycled on Xi'an's ancient wall, and visited the otherworldly Zhangjiajie Mountains, where *Avatar* was filmed. Ana had only one word for Zhangjiajie: "Unbelievable!" She also tried her hand at picking tea, but when she tried to carry a 25 kg basket of tea leaves that a Chinese lady had born effortlessly on her petite shoulders, Ana gave up and said, "I'd better keep my day job."

They also enjoyed the pandas in Chengdu, the futuristic city of Shanghai, the Stone Forest of Kunming, the sobering Nanjing Massacre Memorial Hall in Nanjing, and Hong Kong, which Tom says is "truly where the East meets West and thrives."

Tom and Ana still have many more places they hope to visit, including Harbin, in the north, bordering Russia; Hangzhou, which Marco Polo said was the greatest city in the world; the Wuyi Mountains, home of famous teas and Zhu Xi, father of Neo-Confucianism; Guilin, with the whimsical mountains that inspired Dr. Seuss; and Guangzhou, which even thirteen hundred years ago had some two-hundred-thousand foreign residents from all over the known world.

Ana picking tea in Nanping.

For Ana and Tom, life in China has been a great learning experience. Ana said, "To have the opportunity to know this country, to learn from it, to get out of your comfort zone and to feel great about it, that is priceless."

And Tom added, "China will always have a special place in my heart."

No doubt, many Chinese have a special place in their heart for Tom and Ana.

Ana traveling in Sichuan with friends.

CHAPTER TWENTY

Bill Brown

A Sixty-Year Detour to China

Like so many other Americans in this book, I had no interest in China in my youth. My dream was Australia, but when I applied to emigrate, the Australian Embassy replied that even though they needed men of vision like me, I needed to reapply in ten years because the minimum age was eighteen and I was eight.

But to ease the rejection, they sent me a box of children's books about Australia. Sixty years later, I can still quote the poems about Australian animals.

I then set my heart on Africa, South America, Europe, the Middle East—everywhere but Asia, because in school I'd read nothing about Asia. A lifetime later, when I finally turned eighteen, I saw a poster of the Seychelles in the US Air Force recruiting station's window. I waltzed inside simply to ask where the photo had been taken. I staggered out two hours later, amazed that I'd just enlisted—but with the promise that I'd see the world, and after four years of service, they'd pay four years of college tuition.

After a year of bootcamp and other training, I was raring to see the world, and was sent to Tampa, Florida—only forty miles from home. After a year in Tampa, I was so desperate that I volunteered for Greenland, certain I'd be sent there because no one ever volunteered to be stationed on a block of ice for two years. My friends, meanwhile, all volunteered for the dream assignment—the beautiful island of Taiwan.

But my friends were sent to Greenland and I was packed off to Taiwan. When I learned Taiwan was only a hundred miles from one billion Communists bent on world conquest, I was so certain I'd go to war that I gave my car to my little sister. I did survive Taiwan, but she never returned the car.

Bill Brown in Taiwan in 1977—the inspiration for his determination to visit Mainland China.

Although I had zero interest in Asia, I quickly fell in love with Taiwan. I spent all my free time hiking and biking around the island, visiting farmers and ethnic minorities in the mountains, and helping raise money for a children's hospital. But it was a letter from heaven that set me on a path to China's Mainland.

As I mentioned at the beginning of this book, while walking in a farmer's field, a Mainland balloon rained hundreds of leaflets right on my head (I still have one in my university office). I could not read Chinese, but I was shocked that Mainland farmers so closely resembled those in Taiwan. When I learned that three quarters of the people in Taiwan were related to people on the Mainland, and that many had more relatives on the Mainland than in Taiwan, I thought, "If both sides are Chinese, why are they fighting?"

No Choice but Xiamen

I left Taiwan in 1978, determined to someday visit China's Mainland and learn Chinese. Ten years later, in September 1988, I moved with my wife, Susan Marie, and two small sons, to Xiamen University (XMU). Chinese often ask why I chose Xiamen. And I tell them that XMU was the only university in China that provided dorms to foreign students with families. It was truly *Yuánfèn* ("fate," "destiny"). Sue's parents were American teachers in Taiwan, where she had been born and raised, so we were both delighted to be so close to Taiwan. Xiamen and Taiwan people shared the same dialect, foods, music—it was like coming home! But it was the people that made Xiamen not just home but family.

When XMU told us the cafeteria accepted ration tickets, not cash, but they could not allot rations to a foreign family, I asked, "Then how do we eat?"

The problem was resolved within a few weeks, but in the

meantime, Chinese teachers shared their rations with us. "But you won't have enough for yourself!" I said.

"No, we have plenty!" Months later I learned that even without sharing, they did not have enough—yet they gladly shared the little they had. I wrote home, "Who would not love people like these?"

Although Xiamen was backwards in our eyes, with almost daily water and power outages and poor transportation, the locals were happy because life was better than ever, and they were very optimistic about the future. But being a skeptic, I wondered if farmers' lives were also improving.

In January 1989, only four months after moving to Xiamen, I snuck out of the Foreign Teachers' guesthouse at 5:00 a.m., wearing a blue Chinese coat and a blue cap pulled low over my blonde hair, and rode buses, a tractor, a boat, and walked along narrow paths among rice paddies to remote farming and fishing villages. Not surprisingly, rural developments lagged behind those in cities, but the people were happy and optimistic.

I spent a night with farmers who were friends of an XMU teacher. I was surprised how well such poor people ate. A month later, I learned that they had shared with me the special foods they'd saved for Chinese New Year. I felt terrible, but my friend said, "Being able to share with you made their New Year very special—even though two weeks early."

Just One Year?

I planned to be at XMU for only two years, but as *Yuánfèn* would have it, XMU had just started one of China's first MBA programs, and their one American teacher left suddenly because of family problems. They asked me to take his place, but I refused. "I came to study Chinese, not teach."

"We need you," they said. "You can help us build one of China's best MBA programs!"

I almost laughed. Best in China? Maybe if the program were in Beijing, Shanghai, or Guangzhou—they had all the money and *guanxi* ("connections," "networks"). But on little Xiamen Island? I reluctantly agreed to one year, then a second, and a third, during which I wrote an organizational behavior textbook for China's first Chinese MBA textbook series. It slowly dawned on me that if China achieved even a fraction of its goals to fight poverty, it would help more people than other nation. And if China were to develop peacefully—which was important to both China and my own homeland—it would need to learn international business and economics.

So, I'm still teaching MBA, thirty-seven years later.

Telling China's Story

As soon as we disembarked the eighteen-hour slow boat from Hong Kong to Xiamen in 1988, we saw that China was nothing like the Western media had portrayed it. But family and friends were skeptical when I wrote about the "real China," so I started writing about the Chinese I met, and how we shared similar hopes, dreams, struggles, and fears. Although skeptical about my "real China," my readers were delighted to learn about the "real people." Within six months, over five hundred people were reading my monthly letters, and even six- and seven-year-olds wrote to ask questions about China. But when I wrote articles about China's development, some foreigners angrily said, "Only the coast is developing, not the hinterlands."

"How do you know?" I said. "You've never been there!"

"You've never been there either!" they said. Good point. So, I bought a fifteen-passenger van, converted it into a camper, and, in the summer of 1994, my wife, two small sons, and I drove 40,000 km around China in three months. The roads were so poor that we often drove ten or twelve hours in a day to cover 300 km, but we made it to Inner Mongolia, through the Gobi Desert, over the 16,640-foot pass into Tibet, and back to Xiamen through South China.

The West did lag the coast, yet even in 1994, the pragmatic motto was "Roads First, then Riches." In even the poorest regions, the government was building roads and improving education and medical care. And as in Xiamen, the people were optimistic—though everyone expected it would take forty or fifty years to lift the world's largest population from poverty. In our eyes, we were "planting trees so future generations can enjoy the shade." We never imagined we would enjoy the shade within ten or fifteen years.

In 2013, I was surprised when Xi Jinping told remote Miao minority villagers in Hunan that he thought China could defeat absolute poverty by 2020. To see if Xi's goal was feasible, in 2019, I drove around China again with SMXMU (School of Management at XMU) and New Channel colleagues to see how much had changed. In 1994, the trip had spanned forty-thousand km and taken three months; thanks to better infrastructure, the 2019 trip covered twenty-thousand km and took only thirty-two days. And even in Ningxia, which two decades earlier a UNESCO representative had said was hopeless, the people had new highways and railways, and concrete roads to the doorstep of new, safer homes in remote villages. They also had better education and healthcare, and such reliable internet that even remote Tibetan villagers bought and sold online. At the same time as China had developed, it had recovered ecologically damaged land, reversed desertification, and spent more on new energy and green technology than any had other country. I saw that, long before the UN had set forth its much-lauded Sustainable Development Goals for 2030, China had been pursuing the same goals—with much success but little fanfare.

But what amazed me most about China's success was that it has been both top-down and bottom-up. After all, great leadership is impossible without capable people, and capable people without good leadership are directionless. Over the years, I've recorded dozens of "underdog" stories of Chinese who overcame great poverty to achieve success, and then used their wealth to help others fight poverty.

One of my favorites is Madame Yangying, whom I met in 1997, when I helped start Xiamen International School. She came to XMU at age nineteen, but not as a student. A farmgirl with only four years of education, her dream was to earn twenty yuan a month as an XMU professor's maid and send ten Yuan home to her family. She succeeded, and then sold fish and pork, and opened a credit union. Since then, she has started a biotechnology company and four international schools, and not only supports every retiree in her hometown but has donated tens of millions to improve rural education and fight poverty.

Mr. Lin Zhengjia, who joined me on the twenty-thousand km trip in 2019, was so poor that he did not wear shoes until he was a teen. Like Yangying, he had only four years of education. While digging tunnels with a pickaxe, he thought, "I could do this better." He had villagers join his team, landed a small government contract for a tunnel, and after doing an exceptional job, got larger contracts. He read tunneling books he'd bought from abroad and had translated into Chinese. While driving around China in 2019, he showed me some of the seventy-plus tunnels he had dug, including the world's highest railway tunnel, in Tibet, and China's first undersea tunnel, in Xiamen. And like Madame Yangying, he's spent much of his wealth fighting poverty and improving rural education, as well as making documentaries about China and opening museums in China and abroad.

Bill and his young family in 1988 (on bike) and 1989 (by the water).

I also admire Zhu Qingfu, who as an impoverished farm child dreamed of college but had to walk four hours to school and back each day, and work weekends. He also dreamed of being a photographer, so after joining the army, he spent one month's salary on two rolls of film, borrowed an old camera—and won awards for his photos. Today, he is one of China's top photographers and has photographed everyone from Xi Jinping to my oldest son's wedding. And his impoverished family took advantage of new roads to their remote areas to make and sell furniture, and are now wealthier than their famous son.

One of my favorite stories, however, is of Professor Hu Min, who as a child was almost kicked out of school. A teacher said, "He's young, and we don't know what will happen in his life. Give him one more chance." Hu Min was so moved that he buckled down, went to college at fifteen, became China's youngest associate professor—and then gave up a stellar academic career to start New Channel International Education. He's now called the "Father of IELTS" (the International English Language Testing System), and a leader in modern innovative education—and the man who inspired this book.

Yangying, Lin Zhengjia, Zhu Qingfu, Hu Min, the teachers who shared their ration tickets, the farmers who shared their New Year provisions—who would not fall for such people as these?

But the one person who most encouraged me over years was Xi Jinping, who spent seventeen and a half years here in Fujian Province.

In 1999, after two months in a Hong Kong hospital struggling after cancer surgery, I had doubts I'd survive. I've no idea how our governor Xi Jinping knew I was in the hospital, or why he cared. Though we'd met at government meetings, I was not a rich businessman, investor, or diplomat—just an average teacher.

But he sent two people with flowers to the hospital and wishes that I'd recover quickly and return home. I was so moved that I began exercising and lugging my IV tubes behind me, determined to return "home."

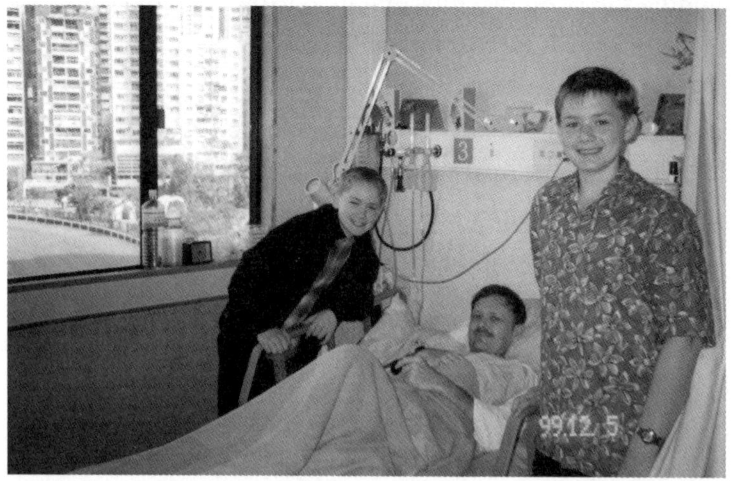

Bill with his sons in the hospital in 1999, where he was recovering after cancer surgery.

Twenty years later, during the March 2019 National People's Congress, Xi had only a few minutes with the Fujian Province delegation, but he took time to ask, "Is Bill Brown retired yet? How is his health?"

I teach leadership and strategy, so I've visited almost every place that Xi has lived to better understand him as a person and as a leader. Without exception, people remember his interest in their personal lives, and his efforts to help them. I believed it, because when he was our governor, he asked me if I had any personal issues that needed help, and he gave me good advice on a family issue.

Most remarkably, people said that Xi never forgot anyone—even remembering a driver's name from forty years earlier. And only recently, one of my friends attended a meeting he had for "old American friends."

Xi said that the people he met in Iowa were, to him, the "real Americans." And for me, Yangying, Hu Min, Lin Zhengjia, and Xi Jinping are the "real Chinese."

Grateful for China and the US

I'm grateful to be American. In spite of our problems, there are reasons that many people want to get an American green card.

At the same time, although I don't understand or agree with all of China's practices, I'm grateful for China and how it has lifted so many people from poverty and is helping many other nations through the Belt and Road Initiative—which is simply exporting its pragmatic and successful "Roads First, then Riches" philosophy. I have many African friends who have told me that their nations did not have much hope until China started to help them build the foundation for development through such practical projects such as highways, railways, dams, airports, and ports, which is simply China's proven "Roads First, then Riches"—export version.

And, not surprisingly, it's not the massive projects but the people-to-people contacts that have most touched Africans' hearts. One African said, "Wealthy Westerners live apart from us and just offer advice as consultants while traveling between air-conditioned offices and air-conditioned homes in air-conditioned cars. But Chinese aren't afraid to get their hands dirty and work with us side by side."

Some 140 years ago, our Fujian governor said the two great powers were China in the East and America in the West. That's still true today. We have different cultures, politics, and economics, but what should unite us far outweighs that which divides us.

Not only China and the US but the entire world will be far better off if we work together—and We the People don't need to wait for politicians to make the first move.